OLIVET DISCOURSE DECODED

Thomas Lynn Burrows

ISBN 979-8-89526-328-0 (paperback)
ISBN 979-8-89526-329-7 (digital)

Christian Faith Publishing
832 Park Avenue
Meadville, PA 16335
www.christianfaithpublishing.com

All biblical citations were taken from the King James Version of the Holy Bible.

Printed in the United States of America

Quote by Timothy LaHaye, coauthor of the
Left Behind books and movies:
"The Olivet Discourse, delivered shortly before Jesus's crucifixion
is the most important single passage of prophecy in all of the Bible.
It is significant because it came from Jesus Himself immediately
after He was rejected by His own people and because it provides
the master outline of the end-times events."

Fig Tree Parable Revealed

A reasonably intelligent understanding of this
long misunderstood riddle or parable,
which shows the year the generation began!

Luke 8:10: "And he said, unto you it is given to know the mysteries
of the kingdom of God; but to others in parables; that seeing
they might not see, and hearing they might not understand."

Luke 8:17: "For nothing is secret, that shall not be made manifest,
neither anything hid, that shall not be known and come abroad."

The Generation Began
September 24, 1950
Black Sunday

The Parable of the Fig Tree

Studying scripture is like putting a puzzle together. If you insert puzzle pieces incorrectly, it prohibits you from completing the puzzle. Future information and studies will need to be corrected if you base them on a misplaced puzzle piece. Let's investigate more historical information about 1950. God confirmed its accuracy:

> And God said, Let there be lights in the firmament of heaven to divide the day from the night; and let them be for signs, and for seasons, and for days, and years. (Genesis 1:14)

> He appointed the moon for seasons: the sun knoweth his going down. (Psalm 104:19)

An amazing event that only God could have created is an eclipse of either the sun or moon—the sun, a solar eclipse, or the moon, a lunar eclipse. Now these happen all the time, mostly partially. The totality of eclipses is more rare but still happens frequently. A rare lunar experience is called a tetrad; this is four total lunar eclipses, each six months apart, over approximately eighteen months.

NASA has a list from Abraham's time, in 2000 BCE. From Abraham to Christ, there have been fifty-six tetrads; from Christ to now, there are fifty-six tetrads; that's 112 tetrads in a four thousand-year period. I studied and have a list from the end of the 1400s till now, and they have occurred at times of great Christian importance. I will include that list, along with their Christian events, in a chapter called "Tetrads." Interestingly, the tetrad of 1949 and 1950 has more associated events than any other tetrad. This is surely confirmation of God pointing out 1950. My lists will show not only signs of the sun and moon but also events like Black Sunday, September 24, 1950. That is what I believe to be a prophecy fulfilling Matthew 24:29. With this being the case, this day of the beginning of the generation is spoken of in verse 34. It would also be the beginning of the transformation of the world as we know it before the tribulation period, where the world will be changed and Jesus, our Messiah, will return. If Christ is in your heart, you believe that Jesus Christ is God, and He came to earth as a human, died, was buried, and rose again. This faith in Jesus Christ is the most important thing to the Lord, and it should reassure and comfort you. Then you have absolutely nothing to fear or worry about. If you do not, this shows time is short for you, and you should humble yourself and worship the Messiah, Jesus Christ, the one and only Messiah, Yeshua. The urgency of this decision cannot be overstated.

The fig tree parable goes like this: "Know the Parable of the fig tree, for when its branch is yet tender and putteth forth leaves; you know that summer is nigh" (Matthew 24:32).

Let's look at this parable and match it up with historical events. On May 14, 1948, the UN proclamation gave Israel the ability and the right to become a nation. However, the ownership of Jerusalem was not theirs, as the UN proclamation gave ownership to the international community. The Jews occupied half of the city, and the Palestinians occupied half of the town, but without ownership of Jerusalem, Israel was not the fig tree. On January 23, 1950, Israel took ownership of the city of Jerusalem entirely, even though they only occupied half of it, and they did this out of faith in God; faith was the most important thing to the Lord. They took ownership and made Jerusalem their capital. Along came 1967, and from June 5 to 10, the Six-Day War took place. The Arab nations attacked Israel for their hatred of the Jewish people. The Arabs were miraculously defeated in six days. Many miracles happened as they acquired pretty much all of the land that the 1948 proclamation had given to the Palestinians. So Israel doubled in size in 1967. This parallels the fig tree parable when "the branch is yet tender and putteth forth leaves."

The fig tree's start would have been on January 23, 1950. The parallel of "the branch was yet tender and putteth forth leaves." is from June 5 to 10 in a six-day war when they doubled their size. If you notice a tree leafing in the springtime, it doubles in size. Then the Lord ends the parable with the words, "Know that the summer is nigh." Now let's look at things we have two verses down from the parable of the fig tree. We have mentioned a generation, and it's almost like when he speaks of the generation, he has already spoken of it in this chapter. Then we look and study and see when he says, "Know that it's summer is nigh." We understand from Psalm 90:10 that a man's life or length of a generation is threescores plus ten (seventy), or if he's a man of strength, eighty. If you take seventy and divide this into four seasons, as a man's life has seasons, we come up with seventeen and a half years per season. So during the Six-Day War, June 5 to 10 is seventeen years and approximately four months from January 23, 1950. The summer of the generation that started in 1950 was nigh or close at hand, as their spring was seventeen and a half years long, a couple of months past the Six-Day War for the summer of the generation to start. This understanding of the fig tree parable earmarks 1950 as the generation's starting point.

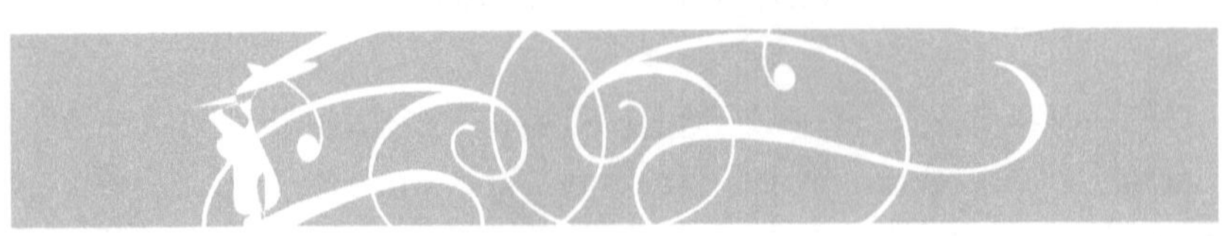

The Olivet Discourse

A quote from Dr. Tim LaHaye, author of the *Left Behind* series, a series of end-times books and movies, "The Olivet Discourse, delivered shortly before Jesus's crucifixion, is the most important single passage of prophecy in all of the Bible. It is significant because it came from Jesus Himself, immediately after He was rejected by His own people, and because it provides the master outline of end-times events."

The Olivet Discourse is located in Matthew chapter 24, Mark chapter 13, and Luke chapter 21. It is the same story that Jesus told to His disciples with some different twists, but with the core story intact in all three gospels. Matthew is probably the most discussed and written-about version. After studying Matthew chapter 24, we find a generation mentioned by Jesus in verse 34. We discovered that if the starting point of that generation were discovered, we would have the starting point of all end-time prophecy. September 24, 1950—is that the starting point? This book is dedicated to showing that proof. Knowing the starting point of the generation and studying a generation's length show you that the word spoken of by Jesus tells us of His on or before the time period of His second coming.

Verse 36 tells us, "But of that day an hour knoweth no man, no, not the angels of heaven. but my Father only."

There is no intent to pick a specific day, nor can that be possible. But an understanding of the parable of the fig tree will show us that the year of the generation is 1950. With further study of events that happened that year, we found some interesting events that happened on September 24, 1950. This day is called *Black Sunday*, and specific events will be discussed in their own chapter. Also, the parable of the fig tree is in its own chapter. I was drawn to study this prophecy because my birthday is September 24, 1950. And the events of that day are a mirror image of the events spoken of in Matthew 24:29: "Immediately after the tribulation of those days shall the sun be darkened, the moon shall not give her light and the stars shall fall from heaven, and the powers of the heavens shall be shaken."

In the beginning of my study, I didn't think this day was this verse because of the word immediately. That referenced a very short time period. Most theologians put the timing of this happening after Christ's second coming, as that's described in verses 27 and 28. With that being the case, a well-known event called the Rapture is not spoken of at all in Matthew 24. But verses 37, 38 and 39 indicate a period of time before the Rapture, as the tribulation period will cause much commotion in the world before Christ's second coming. The world will be looking for its Savior, especially the Jewish people, who will be looking for their Messiah. They missed His first coming. Interestingly, the Jews are looking for Him at the six thousand-year mark on their yearly calendar, as their calendar marks the year from creation to now. Their calendar has a year of 5784 currently. The study of their calendar has a few mistakes that are described by James Ussher in his book *The Annals of the World*. *The Seder Olam* against the Tanakh shows that the six thousandth year has passed and is currently 6028, according to the Tanakh. But the start point of the six thousand years should not be Adam's creation but from when Adam and Eve sinned. These errors in the *Seder Olam* are covered in its own chapter.

Then, when studying the length of the generation biblically, we find in 2 Peter 3:8. "But beloved be not ignorant of this one thing, that one day is with the Lord as one thousand years and one thousand years as one day." This verse clarifies Genesis 2:17, "But of the tree of knowledge of good and evil, thou shalt not eat for in the day that the thou eat of this, that thou shalt surely die." Now we know that Adam and Eve did not die on that day that they ate of the fruit. Humans know a day is a twenty-four-hour period, but they did die within the Lord's understanding or vision of a day. Adam and all pre-flood patriarchs died before they reached one thousand years of age, or a day unto the Lord.

Now in verse 29, we know the Lord is speaking here, and the word *immediately* to Him could be different from our understanding of *immediately*. There was also another disturbing part of verse 29. That was "after the tribulation of that time." These words do not seem to match what is called in the Bible the tribulation period, or the Great Tribulation, or Jacob's trouble, which is Israel's trouble. In the book of Revelation, we see terrible happenings during this time period. Again, the words "after the tribulation of that time" don't come up in the terrible time period known as the Great Tribulation. So seeing September 24, 1950, as being more than five years after World War 2, it better fits "after the tribulation of that time."

Now to tackle the word *immediately* in its meaning, it refers to a short period of time that, though more than five years to us humans, is just 7 and 2/10th minutes to our Lord, making the time period fit the word *immediately*. And verse 29 is fitting to mean the start of the generation spoken of in verse 34, as events on September 24, 1950, match."

"And then" is how verse 30 starts, another period of time, longer than *immediately*. From 1950 to 2025, to our Lord is 1 hour and 48 minutes, a time period that fits "And then," making the rest of the verses 30 and 31 show us the rapture, not a time period after the Second Coming but before the tribulation period. We are now in the winter of the generation and at the end of the time period. And then this makes sense with verses 37, 38, and 39, referencing to the time period before the Rapture.

A verse-by-verse explanation is in order to understand this new explanation of Matthew chapter 24.

Matthew 24:1–2 is a prophecy foretold by Jesus that was fulfilled in history in AD 70 by the destruction of the temple by General Titus of Rome.

Matthew 24:3 is a question Jesus's disciples asked Him about His return. This question is argued quite a bit, but if we concentrate on the answer, we will better understand the question.

Matthew 24:4–51 is what Jesus chose to answer.

Matthew 24:4–8 is a time period for pre-Rapture or time from the beginning of the generation to the Rapture.

Matthew 24:9–14 is the first half of the tribulation period.

Matthew 24:15 is the abomination of desolation prophesied in Daniel 9:24–27.

Matthew 24:16–26 is about things that will happen in the Great Tribulation period, which is the last half of the tribulation period, with its center earmark being the abomination of desolation, also called Jacob's trouble.

Matthew 24:27–28 shows Jesus's Second Coming as the birds will feed on the flesh. Verses 4–28 is a linear narrative, then Jesus jumps back to before verse 4 for the start of the generation, and that was spoken of in verse 34.

Matthew 24:29: is September 24, 1950, the start of the generation?

Matthew 24:30: the first two words, "And then," are the time period that is in verse 4–8.

Matthew 24:30–31: When the time period of "And then" is over, then the rest of verses 30–31 is the Rapture and fits in between verses 8 and 9 and makes sense for verses 37–39.

Matthew 24:32 is the parable of the fig tree, showing 1950 as the year of the start of the generation.

Matthew 24:33: the reason for this book is to wake up to the world to the fact that Jesus is at the door.

Matthew 24:34: the generations verse, which describes the length of time the prophetic chapter 24, verses 4 through 51, when these events will take place.

Matthew 24:35: Promises of the truth of these words, and they will last forever.

Matthew 24:36–38: Describes a somewhat peaceful time, not a tribulation time, that some event will happen in knowing and studying other prophecies. We can surmise that this is the time prior to the Rapture.

Matthew 24:39 shows how shocked the world will be.

Matthew 24:40–41: How people will be taken during the Rapture event.

Matthew 24:42: Be watchful. "But ye brethren, are not in darkness, that that day should not overtake you a thief. Ye are all children of light, and the children of the Day; we are not of the night, nor of darkness. therefore let us not sleep, as do others; but us watch and be sober" (1 Thessalonians 5:4–6)

Matthew 24:43: keep watch; this book is an effort to help.

Matthew 24:44: no man knows the day or hour.

Matthew 24:45–47: this is what this author is trying to do, for our mission is to be a faithful servant.

Matthew 24:48: deniers of the end-times.

Matthew 24:49–51: the judgment of the servant that denies these end-times.

This study has confirmation also. My name being Thomas has me looking at the disciple Thomas, who is called a doubter. With further examination, we find that Thomas just needed confirmation, which he received when Jesus showed Himself to Thomas in the upper room a week after First Fruits Sunday. First Fruits Sunday was the day Jesus was found risen from the dead.

I, like the disciple Thomas, also need confirmation and am dogmatic to search for it, and I will not declare anything as truth without it.

The confirmations I have discovered from the Holy Spirit are the tetrads, my license plate, the many occurrences of biblical numbers in my self and family, the similarities in my family's life and Abram's, my connection to Noah having his name, my nickname at seventeen, and Thomas, which means twin in Hebrew along with my father's age and Methuselah's being divisible by seventeen. Also, being born on the day the generation began indicates God's hand on my life from conception and from the beginning of time to be His servant at His timing. My deep love and devotion to Christ would never let me deceive in any way these findings.

Timothy LaHaye, who I quoted at the beginning of this chapter, has all my respect as a man who was a dedicated servant of God, who pushed the knowledge of the Rapture and was trying to warn the world of what was coming. I have studied for more than twenty-five years from a Timothy LaHaye prophecy study Bible. Timothy gave everyone who helped him in this effort *credit*. Too many authors get other people to do the work, then claim themselves for all the glory. Timothy was a true, humble servant of the Lord. My hope is that this book is just an extension of his work and will again cry out to the unsaved to come to Christ before it's too late.

No fame is being sought here, as it is *Jesus* plus *nothing* equals *everything*. All glory and honor to our Savior, Jesus Christ. I'm merely an extension of God's will to be done.

Matthew 24: Chronological Order

Verses 1–2: Jesus's prophecy of the destruction of the temple fulfilled in AD 70 by Roman General Titus.

Verse 3: the question.

Verse 29: the first day of the generation spoken of in verse 34.

Verses 4–8: time period noted in verse 30 as the "and then" time period.

Verses 30–31: the Rapture.

Verses 9–14: first half of the Tribulation Period.

Verse 15: the abomination of desolation, as prophesied in Daniel 9:27.

Verses 16–26: last half of the tribulation period, Jacob's trouble.

Verses 27–28: the Second Coming of Jesus Christ, our Lord.

Verse 32: the fig tree parable showing 1950 as the generation's beginning.

Verse 33: when you see these things, know the time is nigh.

Verse 34: this generation's verse.

Verse 35: a guarantee from Christ that His words will last.

Verse 36: no man knows the day or hour; not telling us means we are restricted to knowing the season.

Verse 37–39: just as the times of Noah have to be before the Rapture, not the Second Coming.

Verse 40–41: two in the field, what takes place at the Rapture.

Verse 42: watch therefore, for ye know not what hour.

Verse 43: if the good man knew he would watch, calling all good men to watch.

Verse 44: therefore, watch and be ready.

Verse 45: Be a faithful and wise servant, to give meat in due season. The reason for this book!!!!

Verse 46: blessed is that servant that keeps watch.

Verse 47: make him ruler over all his goods.

Verse 48–49: evil servant shall say in his heart, "The Lord delayeth his coming and begin to treat others poor."

Verse 50–51: the Lord will come a day they will not look for Him and cut Him asunder and appoint His portion with the hypocrites.

Verses 4–28 are a linear narrative. as Jesus speaks the story in its chronological order. He left out its beginning and the Rapture. Then in verse 29, He jumps back to the start of the generation spoken of in verse 34, "*this generation.*" The word *immediately* at the beginning of verse 29 to Christ is 7.2 minutes. From 1945 (the end of WWII) and 1950 (the start of the generation), verse 30 starts with "*and then,*" another period of time, but longer than immediately. To Christ, 1950 to 2025 is one hour and forty-eight minutes. Fitting verse 30–31 right after the Pre-Rapture time period, followed by the Tribulation period and Christ's return.

The Generation

The word *generation* of the English language is not as specific as the ancient languages. Case in point: the Greek language has at least eight words for the English word *love*. They are eros, storge, mania, philia, philautia, pragma, ludus, pragma, and agape. All these Greek words mean a different type of love. These eight words define the specific meaning of our one-word love. The English word *generation* also has a multitude of meanings. Whether its context is singular or multiple (layered), each would have an average length, depending on the time period of world creation, which has an extreme effect on its length. *Genea* is one Greek word that is the root word for our generation. *Genea*'s definition is fathered birth, begotten by men of the same stock, a family set of several ranks of natural descent, and the succession of genealogy members.

However, the word *Yevea* was used in the Olivet Discourse in Matthew 24:34 and Mark 13:30. In this context, the translation is "the whole multitude of men living at the same time." Luke 21:32, another version of the Olivet Discourse, uses *Yeveai*, primarily for the Jewish race, who live at one time and at the same time. In all three verses of the discourses, the root word is used, but all are stated singularly. The concept of a "generation" that's layered or multiple generations is a fascinating one, with the time period being the length of all layered families divided by the number of layered families—families that overlapped. A singular *Yevea* would have a starting point and would extend to the average age of a man living at that time.

At the dawn of creation, man was designed to live indefinitely, with no structured time period for this generation. However, with the introduction of sin, as declared by God, "you will surely die," a significant shift occurred. A day to the Lord equates to one thousand years, and the pre-flood patriarchs did not exceed this time frame. Post-flood, the ages of Noah's descendants began to decrease: Shem 603 years, Arphaxad 438 years, Salch 433 years, Eber 464 years, Peleg 239 years, Reu 239 years, Serug 230 years, Nahor 148 years, Terah 205 years, Abraham 175 years, Isaac 180 years, Jacob 147 years, Joseph 110 years, and Moses 120 years.

We see God changing the DNA of men after the flood to decrease their age. Joseph and Moses were men on each side of the captivity in Egypt; according to their ages, a generation would probably be 120 years. Genesis states a man's life to be 120 years. But God was not done working on that DNA. We come to David, where he lived and died at seventy years old. David mostly wrote Psalms, but Psalm 90:10 is unsure of the author: "The days of our years are threescore years and ten, and if by reason of strength, labor, and sorrow is soon cut off, we fly away." Hence, Psalm 90:10 indicates the average age of a man to be seventy to eighty years in length to give God as much room as His and His words as possible. A man is still eighty until he's eighty-one. This average age has pretty much held true from David's time through Jesus's. And Jesus spoke this during the time period, as Psalm 90:10 indicates. I believe that eighty-one would be the greatest number of people living at the same time, per Matthew 24:34. The definition for *Yevea* or *Yeveai*. Notice, this is a certainty. The words "fly away" at the end of Psalm 90:10. Similar to the meaning of the Rapture. The concept of *generation* is also associated with the idea of a sudden and dramatic event that separates the righteous from the unrighteous.

Black Sunday: September 24, 1950

On Black Sunday, September 24, 1950, a significant event unfolded. "Much of the Midwestern United States and Ontario were darkened in the afternoon from noon (Jewish sixth hour) until about 3:00 p.m. (Jewish ninth hour) by thick smoke that had originated from the Chinchaga fire in western Canada. In Cleveland, the early-afternoon baseball game between the Indians and the Detroit Tigers was played with the lights on." This unique occurrence, as described in two books, *Black Sunday* by Betty Masterson Rhodes and *When the Moon and the Sun Turned Blue* by Cody Tymstra, holds profound historical and religious significance. The author of this book, Thomas Lynn Burrows, was born at approximately 1:45 a.m. in North Central Pennsylvania, a city called Lock Haven, which was centrally located as the smoke pall crossed the east coast.

A newspaper article in the *Harrisburg Patriot News* on September 25 covered the event of the 24th. "The Eclipse of the Moon starts at 8:30 p.m. and ends at 2:00 a.m. Celestial phenomena in the area are becoming run-of-the-mill. Saturday night or Sunday morning. It was falling meteorites (stars falling from the sky). Yesterday, there was a pall of smoke, the sky was black from noon till 3:00 p.m., and tonight, there was an eclipse of the moon for sky watchers. The moon will be darkened to a faint copper-red glow tonight (Blood Moon), starting at 8:30 p.m. and concluding at 2:13 a.m. The moon will be in total eclipse from about 10:45 p.m. to 11:40 p.m. If the weather conditions continue as expected, the moon will glow with a queer reddish cast, though the luminary will be entirely in the earth's shadows."

Immediately after the tribulation of those days
shall the sun be darkened, and the moon shall

not give her light, and the stars shall fall from heaven, and the powers of the heavens shall be shaken. (Matthew 24:29)

As my mother told me about the events of this day, I was born. I studied what I could in the history of that day and was drawn to verse 29 in Matthew chapter 24. As a starting point in my studies to find out more, the *Patriot-News* article describes the events that match verse 29. Stars fall from the sky (meteorite shower), the sun is darkened, and the moon shall not give her light. This happened in the time that Jesus had hung on the cross, which was on April 5, AD 30, which was also Nicene 14, where the sky darkened between the sixth and ninth hour, noon to 3:00 p.m., as Christ hung on the cross. This part where heavenly bodies shall be shaken would be genuine, given that this day was the beginning of the transformation of the world as we know it.

Most theologians and students put verse 29 "after" the tribulation period of seven years. As described in Daniel and Revelations, the word *immediately* tends to make that assumption, but the phrase "tribulation of that day" suggests a different context. This was not a significant tribulation period. After a thorough study of the length of a generation and making this discovery in 2 Peter 3:8, "But do not forget this one thing, dear friends: With the Lord, a day is like a thousand years, and a thousand years are like a day." Also, in Matthew chapter 24, we know this is the Lord speaking. So the Lord's meaning of *immediately* was in a different context than ours. September 24, 1950, was a little over five years after World War II, which could have been the tribulation of those days. That five-year period to him would have been 7.2 minutes to our Lord. Which fits the word *immediately*. Verse 30 starts with the words *and then* and describes a longer period than immediately. From 1950 to 2025, it is one hour and forty-eight minutes to the Lord, fitting His *and then*. We are at the end of the period *and then*. The rest of verses 30 and 31 describe the rapture before the tribulation period and the Second Coming of our Lord. This chapter would have no meaning or connection if the Rapture were not stated. In verses 37–39, they talk about, "But as the days of Noah were, so shall the coming of the Son of Man be." The interpretation is that verses 29–31 happened after the tribulation. Verses 37–39 would not fit anywhere. I will include a verse-by-verse interpretation of Matthew chapter 24 that shows the chronological order of the spoken word, demonstrating the thoroughness of our study.

As stated, during my studies that day, I felt the Holy Spirit dropping bits of info like ET and Reese's Pieces in the movie *ET*. The first notable clue was the dates: Black Sunday, the luminary eclipse, and the next day, September 26, the first day of the Feast of Tabernacles, and the last festival of the High Holy Days. These revelations were like puzzle pieces, fitting together to reveal a deeper understanding of the events. It was a clear sign of the divine guidance in my studies—a presence that I hope you can also give in your own spiritual journey.

Jesus referred to Daniel's prophecy of the abomination of desolation in Matthew 24:15, a prophecy in Daniel that defines the Tribulation period in a 490-year prophecy. The Holy Spirit guided me through the parable of the fig tree, evoking the thought of summer as the season of the generation, as spoken of in verse 34. From the outset of this journey, September 24 was the start date of that generation spoken of in verse 34. This personal journey of interpretation and understanding, guided by the Holy Spirit, is a testament to the spiritual connection we can all experience. I invite you to join me in this exploration to deepen your own spiritual connection and understanding of these prophecies and festivals.

My extensive studies of all of God's festivals listed in Leviticus chapter 23 revealed their profound and awe-inspiring significance. Passover, Preparation Day, Nicene 14th, Festival of Unleavened Bread, Nicene 15th to the 21st—these were not just dates but a seven-day festival, where Sunday of the seven-day festival was First Fruits Sunday. This was the day the farmer brought his early barley crop to be waived for God's acceptance, the day Christ was found risen, and the Jews were safe after crossing the Red Sea. Then seven weeks from the First Fruit Sunday would be the Festival of Weeks, which Christians call Pentecost, in the month of Sivan, the third month. Nicene is the first month after God changed the calendar in Exodus chapter 12. Previously, it was the seventh month, and Tishri was the first; now Tishri is the seventh, and Nisan is the first. Then on Tishri 1 and 2, there is Rosh Hashanah, or head of the year or festival of trumpets. Yom Kippur is a day on Tishri 10 where all of Israel, as a nation, sacrifices for its past year's sins. This is the only day of the year that the priest can go into the Holy of Holies, where God meets with him. Then from Tishri 15 to the 21st, is the festival of Tabernacles, a seven-day festival. Then it is the eighth day, called Shemini Atzeret. It is interesting that October 7, last year, when Hamas attacked Israel, was on the eighth day of the Festival Shemini Atzeret.

Mark Biltz, a pastor south of Seattle, Washington, discovered tetrads. I'll write a chapter on these tetrads, which are four lunar eclipses in a row. I noticed in his study that on September 25–26, 1950, the luminary eclipse was the fourth eclipse of a tetrad in 1949 and 1950. Every eclipse landed on a festival day. The 1949 spring eclipse was on Passover; the 1949 fall eclipse was on the Feast of Tabernacles; and the 1950 spring eclipse was again on Passover. In 1950, it fell again on the Feast of Tabernacles. This is also true in known history, especially the Reformation period, a time of great significance in our religious history. And look at all the chapters. Check out the list in the "Tetrad" chapter and edition to the textured in 1949 and 50. In addition to the tetrad, in 1949 and 1950, a total solar eclipse landed on Rosh Hashanah on September 12, 1950.

Tetrads

Tetrad is a word used by NASA to describe four total lunar eclipses in eighteen months, spanning two calendar years. The definition of a *tetrad* is a group of four arrangements. NASA uses this description for a total of four total lunar eclipses. They list them back past the ages of Abraham from 2000 BCE. From Abraham to Christ's time, there have been fifty-six tetrads from Christ's time till now, fifty-six tetrads. That's 112 in more than four thousand years; that's 2.8 tetrads in a century or a hundred years. There are periods of more than three hundred years when tetrads do not occur. We can track back in history, where we can be confident that history is accurate. We notice a fantastic connection with events that were God-inspired to match tetrads.

Let's start in the late 1400s. In 1492, Ferdinand and Isabella retook Spain from the Moors. The Catholic Church agreed with the king in the expulsion of the Jews in Spain during the Spanish Inquisition, and the Spanish king and queen distrusted the Jewish people. The Jewish people were entrenched in the country's economic and financial power, and this new Catholic king and queen demanded the Jews convert to Catholicism or leave Spain, which created a terrible time for the Jewish people in Spain. Many refused to do either. In 1492, an Alhambra Decree was known as the Edict of Expulsion. This mistreatment of the Jewish people by the Catholic Church had gone on since Constantinople, which made Christianity the religion of Rome, putting religious leaders in government positions, which yielded the power of executions. Power corrupts, and absolute power absolutely corrupts. The Catholic Church was behind many expulsions of Jews during AD 1290. The Jewish population of England was expelled. God showed us a sign in the heavens, showing His displeasure with the Catholic Church. There was a tetrad in 1493 and 1494 where all total lunar eclipses landed on God's festivals, Passover and Feast of Tabernacles, and then the next year, again on Passover and the Feast of Tabernacles.

The Catholic Church has historically used its interpretation of Scripture and the limited access of the commoner to the scriptures to maintain control. This is reminiscent of the *Nicolaitans*, a term used in the first couple of letters in Revelation chapters 2 and 3, which refers to those who hold power over the layman. This is made from two Greek words, *nico* (overcomer) and *laitanes* (layman). The hierarchy of the Catholic Church was Nicolaitans, whom Jesus said He hated.

Martin Luther, born before the Spanish Inquisition, was a man prepared by God to challenge this control and lift the thumb of the Catholic Church off the people. His name was Martin Luther, born on November 10, 1483. God molded this man, Martin, who entered the University of Erfurt. From 1501 to 1505, Martin's education was in part to learn Latin, as his father wanted Martin to be a lawyer. On July 2, 1504, Martin got caught in a forest with a lightning storm all around him. His prayer was that if God saved him, he would dedicate his life to God. He was saved, and then, on July 17, 1505, Martin entered the monastery.

Interestingly, there's a tetrad in 1504 and 1505. God is showing His hand to Martin. With his university education complete and his Latin proficiency somewhat intact, Martin started right off reading the Catholic Bible for himself.

Other ministry students without an education in Latin needed the guidance of other monks and priests to interpret the scriptures for them. Martin was ordained to the Catholic priesthood in 1507. He entered Wittenberg University in 1508. His advancement in Wittenberg was quick as he became a professor of theology, teaching students his disagreement with the Catholic Church. In particular, he disputed the view on indulgences. Just like the apostle Paul taught, salvation and eternal life are not earned by good deeds. Instead, they are received only as a free gift of God's grace through the believer's faith in Jesus Christ, and in 1517, Martin posted his ninety-five theses on the Wittenburg front door. Prior to 1517, Martin taught his theological students what was in the ninety-fifth thesis.

There was a tetrad in 1515 and 1516. God's sign was that Martin was God's man. Pope Leo X excommunicated Martin in January of 1521. Prince Fredrick, the founder of Wittenberg, protected Martin from the church's desire to kill him. Prince Fredrick protected Martin from the church by putting Martin in the Tower of Wittenberg. Martin translated the Torah, the first five books of the Bible, and the New Testament into the German language in 1522–1523, giving the everyday person an opportunity to read God's word himself. There was a tetrad in 1522 and 1523, God's sign that Martin was God's man. Martin married Katherine Vaughn Bora in 1525, showing the Scripture to allow Protestant clergy to wed and have a family. Martin sought the assistance of the Jewish community against the Catholic Church, as the church had shown anti-Semitism. He was rejected by the Jews, turning Martin against the Jewish people.

The king of England pursued a divorce from the Catholic Church, presenting the case that he needed an heir. The pope refused; Henry, being a king, didn't like being told no. So he divorced Catherine of Aragon. The pope excommunicated Henry in 1533. Then Henry dismissed the Catholic Church from England and created the Church of England in 1534, making himself head of the Church of England. There was a tetrad in 1533 and 1534. God used many different types of people to fulfill His will. Henry lifted the control of the Catholic Church off the people.

The French Protestant movement in 1562 was a great massacre of the Vassy. This was the murder of French Huguenots, worshippers, and citizens by the troops of the duke of Guise in Vassy, France. This was the first significant event of the wars of religion. Then in 1563, after many battles, the Peace of Amboise was signed, a peace treaty. There was a tetrad in 1562 and 1563, indicating God's recognition of this trouble. All these tetrads indicate God's anger against the Catholic Church for her dominance and control over His loved ones.

The *Book of Concord*, also known as the *Lutheran Confessions*, is the historic document standard of the Lutheran Church. It was affirmed and officially published on June 25, 1580, although some copies are dated 1581. The last tetrad in the 1500s was between 1580 and 1581. God gave His approval to this book.

Let's do a recap:

> 1493 and 1494: we had the banished expulsion of Jews.
>
> 1504 and 1505: we had Martin Luther's commitment to God.
>
> 1515 and 1516: we have Martin Luther teaching his 95 theses.
>
> 1522 and 1523: Martin Luther translated the Torah and New Testament.
>
> 1533 and 1534: God used Henry VIII to throw the Catholic Church from England.
>
> 1562 and 1563: the massacre of Vassy and the peace treaty of Amboise.
>
> 1580 and 1581: the *Book of Concord.*
>
> No tetrads in the 1600s, 1700s, or 1800s.

Tetrads in the 1900s and 2000s

After 326 years of absence of tetrads, the Scofield Bible appeared in 1909 and 1910. The *Scofield Bible* was published in 1909. The study Bible, with its unique interpretation of biblical prophecy, is said to be responsible for making evangelical Christians supportive of Israel and the Jews. This support is rooted in the belief that the reestablishment of Israel as a nation fulfills biblical prophecy, particularly about the end-times. After almost 1,900 years since the crucifixion of Christ and the Catholic Church being very anti-Semitic, things changed in the true Christian community. We're treating Israel as Christians should have been for years. The Jews, or Israel, are the bride of the Father, Yahweh. God shows His hands on these events through His signs in heaven.

The 1927 and 1928 tetrads were a warning for the 1929 crash. With no significant events related to Christianity or Jews, I believe this was a warning from God of the upcoming worldwide economic crash that crippled the US and the world for the next eleven years and was the crutch that Germany used to make a play for total world domination and World War II, which God used to reinstate Israel as a nation and show the USA as the dominant world power. This economic crash, preceded by a tetrad, can be seen as a divine warning of the impending hardship, a concept consistent with biblical prophecy. The war effort indeed brought us out of that economic depression.

Now the events of 1949 and 1950. There was a tetrad in 1949 and 1950, in which, like the 1492 and 1493 tetrad, the eclipses all landed on God's festivals of Passover in the spring and Tabernacles in the fall. Then in 1950, there were solar eclipses at God's festival of Rosh Hashanah on September 11 and 12. It was strange for it to be listed on two days, but the eclipse was on the International Date Line—Alaska on the 11th and Russia on the 12th—on the same day. It is interesting to notice strange events. In June of 1949, Billy Graham started his crusade in Los Angeles, and as I have heard the story, Billy asked the Lord for a sign of an amount of money to be given. An envelope with thousands of dollars showed up at Billy's hotel, fulfilling what he had asked the Lord to give him as a sign. Probably the most excellent deliverer of the gospel ever since the apostle Paul.

Then in October of 1949, the prime minister of Israel, Benjamin Netanyahu, was born. God brought this man up for this very occasion as the end-times. On May 14, 1948, Israel was granted the right by the UN to have a nation, with the UN dictating the land the Jews should occupy and also the land that Palestinians should occupy. The ownership of Jerusalem was not by either one but by the international community. The Jews occupied half of Jerusalem, and the Jordanian Palestinians occupied the other half. Neither owned any part of it. Then on January 23, 1950, the Knesset of Israel, out of pure faith in Yahweh, made a proclamation to take ownership of Jerusalem and called Jerusalem their capital. This was a crucial step in faith in God and made Israel a complete nation, which, at the time, could be called the *fig tree*. With Jerusalem, it was the *fig tree*.

Later, on September 24, 1950, an event called Black Sunday—the event of this day, I believe—is listed in prophecy in Matthew 24:29. This prophetic verse was fulfilled on this day. I have a whole chapter on Black Sunday. On September 25, in the evening, the last total eclipse of the 1949–1950 tetrad happened. Then September 26, 1950, was the first day of the Feast of Tabernacles. Jesus pointed to Daniel's prophecy in Matthew 24:15, which was the prophecy of the abomination of desolation. That prophecy and Daniel are in 9:24–27. This matches the dates of events in September. 24–26 of 1950, but nothing at 9:27 in 1950; something will happen later.

The Six-Day War happened in June 1967, from the 5th to the 10th. Israel was attacked by the Arab nations. Israel defeated these nations, even though they were outnumbered. Many miracles happened during this conflict, where Israel doubled in size and took over all of Jerusalem. And in the parable of the fig tree, this is where the branch was yet tender and putteth forth leaves. I'll address this in a chapter of its own. The year 1968 was the season division of the generation that started in September of 1950, ending its Spring and starting its Summer. In the parable of the fig tree, the ending says, Know that summer is nigh, or close at hand. All the lunar eclipses landed on festival days—Passover and Tabernacle, both years.

In 1985 and 1986, another tetrad. This tetrad marks the season change of the generation that started in September of 1950. This tetrad marks this season's change from summer to fall then fall to winter in 2003–2004; this tetrad marks the change in the generation's season that started in September 1950. All these tetrads mark the season changes of the generation.

> He appointed the moon for seasons; the sun knoweth his going down. (Psalm 104:19)

> But of the times and the seasons, brethren, ye have no need that I write unto you. For yourselves know perfectly that the day of the Lord so cometh as a thief in the night. For when they shall say, Peace and safety; then sudden destruction cometh upon them, as travail upon a woman with child; and they shall not escape. But ye, brethren, are not in darkness, that that day should overtake you as a thief. Ye are all the children of light, and the children of the day: we are not of the night, nor of darkness. (1 Thessalonians 5:1–5)

Four tetrads, all with sixteen years separating each. As we look back in time to Abraham, there occurred one other time that four tetrads in a row, each sixteen years apart, happened. This separated the seasons of the generation that started in 1950 and is the confirmation of God that this earmarks the generation that the Lord talks about in Matthew 24:34.

Donald Trump's tetrad is one last tetrad, which completes the total tetrads to fifty-six after Christ and fifty-six between Abraham and Christ. This occurred in 2014 and 2015, with all eclipses landing on festivals. In June of 2015, Donald Trump announced he was running for president of the US. This tetrad sign signifies that God had His hand on Donald for God's purposes and will. Donald Trump was successful in the 2016 election and was sworn in in January 2017. Donald's job was to shine a light on the evil in our government. Moses shined the light on Pharaoh; the prophets shined the light on the Israelites; Christ shined the light on the Pharisees for their evil arrogance of looking holy, for which He was killed; and Martin shined the light on the Catholic Church for its control of the people. Now, last but not least, Donald J. Trump has shed light on the evil in our press, the FBI, the CIA, and most importantly, the Democratic Party. Then we need to show how good Donald Trump was. God brought on Joe Biden. Joe eliminated all the good that Donald had done. He stopped oil exploration, driving the price of oil up, enriching our enemies, Iran and Russia, and bringing on inflation. To add insult to injury, he opened the border. The man's whole career has been based on deceit. His father is Satan, as are the Pharisees.

The last eclipse of the 2014–2015 tetrad was on 9/27, or September 27, the last verse in Daniel's prophecy of the abomination of desolation. The first three verses (9:24–26) happened in 1950.

Let's do a recap:

> 1909–1910: *Scofield Bible* published
> 1927–1928: warning of 1929 crash
> 1949–1950: Billy Graham, Netanyahu's birth, Jerusalem became capital, solar eclipse on Rosh Hashanah on September 12 and Black Sunday on September 24, last lunar eclipse on September 25, the Feast of Tabernacles September 26, dates 9/24–26 match Daniel's prophecy of abomination of desolation spoken of by Christ in Matthew 24:15

1967–1968: Six-Day War 1967, split of generations seasons, spring to summer

1985–1986: split of generations seasons summer to fall

2003–2004: split of generations seasons fall to winter

2014–2015: Donald Trump's tetrad with the last eclipse on September 27 or 9:27, the last verse in Daniel's prophecy that earmarks the seven-year Tribulation period.

Parables and Types

Jesus, a master of parables, used this powerful form of storytelling to convey profound truths. The presence of parables in the Old Testament, a common feature in Jewish communication, is a significant sign that Jesus was deeply rooted in His Jewish heritage.

The Old Testament has stories of biblical figures with prophetic parabolic meanings—called types. We get the name from the Greek word *parabole*, which means comparison. The geometric figure parabolic refers to a curve shaped like a path of something thrown up and forward, high in the air, and falling back to the ground. This action creates an arched figure with two identical sides.

Jesus said in Luke 8:10–15:

> And he said, "Unto you, it is given to know the mysteries of the kingdom of God: but to others in parables; that seeing they might not see, and hearing they might not understand. Now the parable is this: The seed is the word of God. Those by the wayside are they that hear; then cometh the devil, and taketh away the word out of their hearts, lest they should believe and be saved. They on the rock are they, which, when they hear, receive the word with joy; and these have no root, which for a while believe, and in times of temptation fall away. And that which fell among thorns are they, which, when they have heard, go forth, and are choked with cares and riches and pleasures of this life, and bring no fruit to perfection. But that on the good ground are they, which in an honest and

good heart, having heard the word, keep it, and
bring forth fruit with patience."

As Christ's example shows, every detail of the parable has an equally related answer or conclusion. This is an example with a parallel meaning. It could also be a parallel between history and the types of essential parables. First, we have the life of Joseph as a parallel story of Christ. Joseph's story encompasses fifteen chapters in Genesis out of fifty. A little over one-quarter of Genesis is all about Joseph from chapter 37, where Joseph is seventeen years old. He had dreams that depicted himself as ruling over his brothers and father. This brought anger from them all. Joseph was an innocent young man who was only searching for answers. This period parallels Joseph's brothers and the Jews to Jesus's teaching period with His disciples and His interaction with the Pharisees. The Pharisees despised His miracles and His declaring He was the Son of Man or God, to the point they wanted him killed, the same as Joseph's brothers. Joseph's brothers put him in the ground, a hysteron or well, which parallels Christ being in the heart of the earth. For three days and three nights, Joseph was taken to Egypt, where, at thirty, he met the Pharaoh, who made Joseph the ruler of Egypt. Christ started His ministry at thirty years old, then at thirty-three was killed, rose again, and returned to heaven, where He is ruler. This period of Joseph is symbolic of Christ. Rejection from his brothers during his first coming. His brothers coming to Egypt during the seven years of famine is a symbolic future prophecy of the seven-year tribulation period where the Jews, like Joseph's brothers, will come to Jesus and recognize that He is and was the Messiah, as Joseph's brothers recognize him as their savior. God engineers all.

Joseph's dream of superiority.	Jesus's superiority to the Pharisees.
Joseph's brothers wanted to kill him.	Christ's brothers, the Jews, killed Him.
Joseph is in the well.	Jesus is in the heart of the earth.

Joseph, at thirty, meets Pharaoh.	Christ, at thirty, starts His ministry on earth.
The Pharaoh chose Joseph as ruler of Egypt.	Christ in heaven is our ruler.
Joseph's brothers seek help during the famine.	The Jews will come to Christ in the seven-year tribulation
Joseph loved and forgave his brothers.	Christ loves and forgives the Jews, the Father's Bride.

Other types are Abraham, Sarah, Isaac, Eliezer (Abraham's servant), and Rebecca. The Abrahamic covenant was a marriage covenant with God. Abraham is symbolic of God the Father, Yahweh. Sarah was Abraham's wife, symbolic of the Jewish people from whom Christ came, whereas Sarah's son, Isaac, is symbolic of Christ the Messiah, Abraham's begotten son, and Christ is God the Father's begotten son. Abraham's servant, Eliezer, was sent to find a bride for Isaac. Eliezer, which means God's helper or Holy Spirit. Jesus sent the Holy Spirit at Pentecost to find the church (a body of believers with Christ as their husband or head). He located Rebekah, Abraham's brother's granddaughter, to be Isaac's bride, just as the church, being the body of believers, will be Christ's bride. We will be adopted into the family of God.

Abraham	Yahweh, God the Father
Sarah, the wife of Abraham	the Jewish people, the Bride of Yahweh
Isaac, the begotten son	Jesus, the begotten Son of God
Eliezer (God's Helper), Abraham's servant	the Holy Spirit
Rebekah, Isaac's bride	the body of believers, the church

- These types and parables should touch the hearts of the Jewish people who do not believe in Christ as the Messiah. They are also confirmation that only God, in His all-knowing, that He and He alone could have laid this out so perfectly. All praise and honor go to our Lord and Savior, Jesus Christ.

The fig tree parable as the Lord has shown me:

- The fig tree started in 1950 as Israel took ownership of Jerusalem and made it whole.
- The branch yet tender and putteth forth leaves 1967, the Six-Day War.
- Know that summer is nigh. The summer of the generation starting in 1950 was nigh.

Biblical Numbers

I started seeing specific numbers evident and frequent in my family: seven, thirteen, seventeen, eighteen, and twenty-four. These are the numbers that occurred frequently. The Holy Spirit, I believe, brought me a book called *Biblical Mathematics* by Ed Vallowe, a pastor and devoted disciple who scoured the scriptures for these meanings. I always recognized twenty-four as a frequent number in that my birthday and my brother's birthdays were on the twenty-fourth, as my oldest brother. My Social Security number ends in twenty-four. My father was married at twenty-four. I was married at twenty-four. The number twenty-four, biblically, has the meaning of priesthood. There were twenty-four sections of the Levites to serve the tabernacle or temple during the feast days and the entire year.

Seventeen is a number that indicates victory. My oldest brother was killed on August 17, 1960, at fourteen years of age—a week from being fifteen. Jesus was crucified on the fourteenth of Nisan and almost the fifteenth. Then my middle brother died of a heart attack on January 17, 2017. This is when I started looking at these numbers, as there were too many for them all to be coincidences. I started looking back for other things. My football teammates nicknamed me *Noah* just after I turned seventeen. My wife, Pat, and I lived for seventeen years on the West Coast, in Tahoe for twelve years, and in Reno for five years. We then moved to northeast Georgia, where Pat found a house she loved. I was a little skeptical because of the future expenses the house would need. We bought the house, and the seventeen-mile marker is right next to our driveway on Route 76 outside of Hiawassee. Another example of seventeen is my family as well as myself. My brothers and I, Larry Dayne Burrows and Richard Lee Burrows, have seventeen letters in our names. The biblical meaning of victory is the number seventeen. My first marriage was on May 17, 1975. Seventeen is the seventh prime number, and seven means perfect completion, and with that comes seventeen or victory.

September 24, 1950, which was Black Sunday, was also Tishri 13—right between the tenth Yom Kippur and the fifteenth, the Feast of Tabernacles. My mother's birthday is June 13, 1920. My father died on December 13, 1986. Thirteen, biblically, means destruction or depravity. Thirteen is the sixth prime number, and six means Satan, or "man without God." With six, or "man without God," comes destruction or depravity. That is what Noah preached for 120 years as he built the ark. I feel that the nickname *Noah* defines my job, which is preaching that destruction is coming. A confirmation that God showed me was that *Noah's* grandfather, Methuselah, aged 969, was divisible by seventeen and the only pre-flood patriarch. The Lord's confirmation to me is that my father's age of sixty-eight is divisible by seventeen. I just love these confirmations. My name, Thomas, in Hebrew means *twin*.

The number seven is frequent in my life, being born on September 24, nine months from Christmas. My question to my mother was, "Was I conceived on Christmas?"

She answered, "No. You were an anniversary baby because your father and I were married on December 26, 1942, a war bride."

So 1949 would have been my parent's seventh wedding anniversary, of which I was conceived. I was born in Lock Haven, Pennsylvania. And just as I turned seven, my family moved to the Hummelstown/Hershey, Pennsylvania, area. I entered second grade after school had started, sometime at the beginning of October. We moved because of my father's employment. Westinghouse hired him out of Harrisburg, Pennsylvania. I started an electrical contracting business in the spring of 1994. I then retired after seven years in 2001. I bought a 1774 farmhouse in Palmyra, Pennsylvania, in 2004. I remodeled it, lived there till 2011, then sold it for a seven-year period. I bought what I called the barn in 1997. I purchased the property for my electrical contracting business. It was a farm property with a farmhouse split into two rentals—a barn where antiques were sold by antique dealers that rented space. A pizza restaurant was in the old corn barn. I fixed up a remodeled chicken coop for my office. The man I purchased the property from continued to run the antique barn but wanted out of it. I paid him for his equipment—a register, etc. I started running the antique barn along with my contracting business. One of the dealers in the barn became my wife and best friend, Patricia, a widow, as her first husband had died of brain cancer. We remodeled the barn for a gift shop for Pat, then eventually sold it to the family with the pizza shop. Fabio's, an Italian restaurant, moved into Pat's gift shop in the barn. We sold the barn in 2004. We have had the property for seven years.

Eighteen is the remaining number that was significant only to me. I separated from my first wife on the Monday before Easter in 1993. This was also Nicene 14 preparation day for Passover. The day Christ was crucified. It was also on April 5, both calendar days, that in AD 30 Christ was crucified. It's interesting that when I left my first wife, her first words were, "Oh my God, I'm going to be poor." She wasn't interested in telling me she loved me. Then on the Monday before Easter 1994, the same day related to Easter in both years, on March 28—also Nicene 16, the second day of the festival of unleavened bread—I was terminated from employment at the Edwin L. Heim Company. I previously had eighteen years of service with them. The number eighteen, biblically, means freedom from bondage, or a period of time of bondage. I had freedom from bondage, from both.

Biblical Mathematics by Dr. Ed Vallowe, I recommend to anybody seriously studying scripture to find this book. It will bring true meaning to your study and your life. I'll list the first thirty numbers from Dr. Ed's book, but you need to get the book to understand how Ed gleaned the scripture.

- 1–unity
- 2–union, division
- 3–resurrection, Trinity, divine completeness
- 4–world, creation
- 5–grace
- 6–man without God, Satan

- 7–perfect completion of time
- 8–new beginning
- 9–fruits of the Spirit
- 10–law, commandments
- 11–judgment, disorder
- 12–government
- 13–destruction, depravity
- 14–salvation
- 15–rest
- 16–*love*
- 17–*victory*
- 18–bondage and freedom of bondage
- 19–faith brings new beginning
- 20–redemption
- 21–offspring
- 22–light
- 23–death
- 24–priesthood
- 25–hope
- 26–the gospel
- 27–preaching gospel
- 28–eternal life
- 29–departure
- 30–the *blood of Jesus Christ*

Miracle and Confirmation

We had our house in Reno up for sale for about a year. It sold right after our seventeenth anniversary of living on the West Coast. The number seventeen has always held special significance in our family. It symbolizes victory biblically.

This number has been a guiding force in our lives. We prepared with a forty-foot RV rigged up to pull our 2008 Ram pickup. We left as soon as we settled on 2335 Eagle Bend Trail, Reno, Nevada, a house I had built from 2013 to 2015. It's where we lived for three years before selling. A miracle happened while building this house. We designed it to fit into the desert landscape with a post-and-beam construction in the center structure and main hall, with both sides of the home being framed out like a normal house. I had purchased a quantity of a hundred 8" by 16" by 16 foot-long Douglas fir reclaimed timbers with the thought of building this house with recycled timber. That was a trend at the time. The neighborhood was upscale and required an architect or licensed home designer and structural engineer to do their thing with earthquake construction.

The engineer, a crucial part of our project, was given the sizes and approximate grades of my reclaimed lumber. He finished and put in the timber sizes I had. He, unfortunately, put a note on the drawings that they needed to be number one grade and free of heart center. Well, this was not the grade of timber I had. I had probably number two grades, and they weren't free of heart center. I contacted the engineer about this note on my drawing. As surely, this was a CYA or "cover his butt" note. Asking him to take the note off, he refused, saying the inspectors would never look at that. I wouldn't put all this effort into constructing this home with these timbers when they might make you tear it down, as they would not meet drawing specifications.

This information bothered me as we began this project with footers and basement walls. We started because we didn't need the timbers until all the foundation and side framing were close to complete. But this problem was definitely on my mind, and at some point in time, I had to address this problem.

Then when the timing had come to the point where I needed to decide what to do, my budget was tight, and this timber was probably a fifty-thousand-dollar addition. Then, on Craig's List, a tractor-trailer load of Doug fir timber, number one grade free of heart center, came up for sale for $5,000. I never checked the total value of this timber, but I estimate it to be close to $50,000. The timber was more significant in size than what the engineer had designed the house to be. Then we went to look at the timber, and being a contractor and a little bit foolish, I tried to get the timber for even less than $5,000, offering $4,500, of which the gentleman I was talking to was not the timber owner, and he said he would get back to me. It was on a Saturday that we looked at the timber and were going to our son's house in Sacramento. The timber was in Truckee, California. On Sunday, I got up thinking that I was foolish. The Lord had put this right before me—what I needed. I was a bit blockheaded and trying to shave off $500 from something I needed badly. I contacted that gentleman on Sunday and told him to forget about that $4,500 offer, that I would be willing to pay the $5,000 and consider the tractor-trailer load sold, and that I would deliver a check to the timber owner in Reno on Monday morning.

After the timber was delivered, I wasn't sure if the sizes would be suitable, but I knew they were larger than I needed and would need to be sawed. We had the load delivered to the jobsite so it could be investigated as to what sizes I needed and to maximize getting all I needed out of this purchase. I unloaded it on the side of the road and began figuring it out. I had a twenty-four-foot-long bandsaw, so I was prepared to cut these timbers as needed. So I cut these timbers to the 8x16x16-foot extended sizes I required. I looked at the sizes and tried to determine the best way to get the most out of what I had. And not knowing, even now, whether I had enough, needed to purchase more, or maybe have some left over. We cut the timber and got all of our pieces in the main house done.

We had a lot of 4 x 16 timber that was off 12 x 16 timber that the engineer left me to bolt together for the timber needed for our deck. It was also designed around 8 x 16 timber. This allowed me to complete our project to the correct timber sizes. The deck timbers weren't as structurally critical. I contacted the engineer, and he allowed me to do this. I was trying to use every piece of material I could. We completed the house, and there was not one scrap of timber left, and every piece of timber in that house was completed. I did not have to buy one more significant piece of timber for that house. Now tell me that was not God, knowing what I needed before I needed it. This experience brought me a sense of relief and reassurance, knowing that God had provided exactly what I needed when I needed it.

The timber came from a bank project that was being built in Reno, Nevada, and whether or not the timber was over-ordered or whether there were some changes in the bank to make this timber available. I do not know, but I do know the Lord was in charge of it. And the blessings that He has given me throughout my life are amazing, this being one of them. This experience was a testament to the fulfillment and gratitude that come from witnessing God's hand in our lives, guiding us and providing for us in ways we could never have imagined. It was a journey of faith and trust, and it deepened my spiritual connection with God.

We then moved from Reno to Hiawassee, Georgia, at the end of 2018. We found a house, purchased it, and settled on it on February 28, 2019. Moving to a new state meant we needed a new driver's license and vehicle license plates. I was a bit upset about the VAT tax in Georgia and decided that rather than paying it on the Lexus I was bringing in, I decided to sell that vehicle and make a deal to lease a new Lexus. We had a 2015 RX 350 Lexus and found the same color in 2019. And we were able to make a deal on leasing that, where I paid that sales tax every month rather than on a big lump sum. So to end that story, we needed to get license plates, and the license plate was pulled right off the pile. I've never paid for a special plate, and this was no exception. The given license plate came right off the top of the pile. The plate was CAM1950.

At that time, I was praying to the Lord to show me or confirm what I thought He was showing me to be true. Now 1950 is the year of my birth and the year that the fig tree parable shows as the beginning of that generation. This book is being written because September 24, 1950, my birthday, is the beginning day of the generation spoken about in Matthew 24:34. I recently learned from some studies that the first three letters, *cam* was the Greek word used for Joseph of Arimathea to go into Pilate boldly. So *go boldly* is the translation of the Greek word *cam*. So I take it that my Lord was telling me that I needed to go boldly and tell the world about 1950 and what it represents in Scripture—what the world is yet to see and should prepare for. The beginning of the transformation of the world has begun!

Author's Bio

Why did God reveal this info to the author, Thomas Lynn Burrows, and what evidence is there that God's hand has been on Thomas since his conception and even before? First of all, Thomas's birthday is the day called Black Sunday, which I believe is the beginning of the generation spoken of in Matthew 24:34. In a study of Thomas's life, we begin way back at Thomas's parents' birth. His father, Donald C. Burrows, has a birthday in the same month as Billy Graham, the most profound preacher ever to take the world stage during the time of TV and worldwide communications. Billy was born on November 7, 1918, and my father on November 30, 1918. My mother was born in the same month and year as Ruth Graham, Billy's wife. Ruth was born on June 10, 1920. My mother was born on June 13, 1920. My parents were married on December 26, 1942.

As a war bride, my father was headed off to war for training. He enlisted in the army air force and was scheduled as a B-17 engineer and top turret gunner. He bombed in the Normandy invasion and the Naples invasion. He bombed Germany, Berlin specifically, and the Croatians, where he was flying out of Italy, and was shot down over Romania. He was a POW. For a couple of months, he returned home to father my oldest brother, who was born on August 24, 1945. Then another brother was born on November 3, 1946. So Dad had been home by November of 1944. Before the war ended, he was sent home after being liberated from prison. My parents moved from Butler County, Pennsylvania, ironically, the same town where President Trump recently had his life threatened; an assassin tried to take his life.

My father and family moved to Lock Haven, Pennsylvania, for employment. Dad received employment with Piper Aircraft sometime in 1947. I was conceived on December 26, 1949; this was my parents' seventh wedding anniversary. I know this because I asked my mom after Dad had passed, "If I was a Christmas baby or if I was conceived on Christmas?" My birthday, September 24, makes Christmas pretty close to that nine-month mark.

She responded, "No, you were an anniversary baby. We were married on December 26, and it was on our anniversary that you were conceived."

God's number system is quite profound, with the seventh being a number of perfection, a completion of time. Throughout the Bible, we see that. We lived in Lock Haven, and right after my seventh birthday, my father received employment from Westinghouse Corporation in the Harrisburg, Pennsylvania, area. This would have been around October of 1957. We moved to a farmhouse outside of Hummelstown/Hershey, Pennsylvania. This country's farmland was a great place to grow up: amazing friends, good schools, and wonderful Christian neighbors. We first rented a farmhouse whose previous occupant was a retired farmer, whom my parents befriended and who was responsible for the church I grew up in. We moved to two other rural rental homes before my dad could purchase the farmhouse we had initially rented. This is where I claim to have grown up—the retired farmer whose name we call Grandpa Saufley.

My elementary and high school years were very rewarding, as we had many wonderful teachers and mentors. I grew a good bit between my freshman and sophomore years in high school. I grew six inches that summer and slimmed down from an average height and a little bit chunky to 6'2" and around 210 pounds. I was just suitable for football, which I grew to love. In my senior year, when I was seventeen, my teammates gave me the nickname "Noah." This was also one of God's signs of His purpose for me. Seventeen is also an amazing number in the Bible. Interestingly, this did not happen till I was seventeen. We were starting our senior season and about four to five games into it when we returned to the high school on our bus; it was raining hard. I had a 1949 Mercury that took many players home after practice. The largest number we remember was eighteen guys in my car. The car looked like an upside-down bathtub, which was called the "ark" that night. And I, the driver/owner, became Noah. I attended college in the fall after high school graduation, playing football and working part-time. I respected my high school teachers and thought I might become one. With math as my favorite subject and football as my favorite sport, I planned to be a math teacher and football coach. I realized my father was struggling to pay for my college education even while I was working, so I quit school and started working in construction. The Monday after Thanksgiving in 1968, I started a job at Three Mile Island, a nuclear power plant. I had worked summers framing houses and also for an insulating company. As a farm boy, construction seems to be the appropriate life path.

I married at the age of twenty-four on May 17, 1975. At the time, I was working as a laborer. I decided to pursue a better-paying trade. I was accepted into the electrical apprenticeship program of the IBEW, for which I was accepted, but we didn't start working till after I was twenty-six because of a year of very slow employment. I served four years as an apprentice, where I was one of the oldest apprentices. Most started at the age of eighteen. With my seven years of previous experience in construction, I showed a bit more knowledge and experience than my fellow apprentices. As an apprentice, I was even asked to handle small jobs as the lead person or foreman. I had to acquire a humble attitude and not piss off the journeyman. I finished the apprenticeship at the age of thirty. I then started working right away on my company's largest account, *Weis Markets*, a 150-store chain at the time. I started by installing the first scanner registers in the country—three stores at first and then many more—as this new technology eliminated a lot of labor. When we installed all the scanner registers they wanted, my workmate and my best friend, Bruce Wolf, started installing energy management systems in the stores. This technology saved a lot of electricity costs. The electric bill for a supermarket, which included refrigeration and lighting costs, was one of its most significant expenses. Energy management systems were installed in these stores to reduce these costs.

Bruce and I became friends with the Weis employees we worked for. We also became acquainted with their many stores and store managers. I was picked from the two of us to go into the office of Edwin L. Heim Co. and learn supervision and estimation. The vice president was retiring from Heim, who had acquired the Weis account. His successor, Homer Myers, was taking his place, and his position of designing and supervising that account was then handed off to me. These tasks would be undertaken in the first four days of the week. Friday was the day to visit Weis Markets, meet all the various individual clients, and meet with Robert Weis himself. As a thirty-two-year-old without proper engineering education, I took on this task. I was a bit timid about interacting with Robert at first. You have to understand that Robert was fifty-first on the Forbes 500 list and needed to be given service he couldn't get anywhere else to keep and maintain this account. Robert was an amazing man—kind, caring, and appreciative of what he saw you doing for him. I grew to appreciate this man tremendously. I admired him far more than my own bosses. It was a twelve-year span of working for Robert, and looking back, there was a spirit that connected us both. Robert was active in his Jewish faith to the point where he provided funds for Yale University, Susquehanna University, and Franklin and Marshall College for their Jewish studies. Robert and I were serving the same God, Yahweh.

I was not a happy man in my marriage. I felt no love in it. I had two wonderful sons whom I've loved unconditionally. Then on the Monday before Easter in 1993, we separated. We were going through a divorce proceeding, and I was searching for my previously lost Christian faith. I say God grabbed the back of my neck, and I believe I still have the marks He left. But no, seriously, I started taking a stand against my company's policies. Like most commercial contractors, there was a thieving mentality. I saw that the company had lost some accounts by getting caught, and I wanted to avoid this with Weis Markets. I started presenting my case to some personnel. My immediate boss, Homer Myers, had divorced his wife some six to eight years prior to mine. I watched Homer hide finances from his wife in several ways. He presented to me that Barb, now his ex-wife, he thought was emotionally unstable and might commit suicide. When I asked how he knew this, he advised me that she hadn't paid her real estate taxes in four years. He acted like he would be her great savior by paying the taxes for her. I knew all along of his theft of her, and I told him he needed to give her back all that he stole from her, and she could then pay for her own taxes. He did not like my response, and in two weeks, I was terminated. This happened on the Monday before Easter in 1994, a year from the same day associated with Easter as when I separated from my first wife the previous year.

I started Thomas L. Burrows Incorporated as an electrical contractor in 1994, where I worked out of my house to get started. Then I searched for a property to conduct my business. I found a renovated farm with a rental to pay my mortgage, a farmhouse split into two rentals, an antique co-op barn, and a pizza restaurant. There were a few other buildings, one for my office and a warehouse space at the end of the barn for the contracting business. I was blessed to meet my next wife at the antique barn, where she was an antique dealer. A true gift from God.

We married on June 26, 1999, when I was forty-eight years old—two times twenty-four. In 2001, Pat, my wife, and I decided to close my electrical business and retire from 1994 to 2001, which was seven years. We also bought a second house in Lake Tahoe, as my wife's children lived in California, one in Sacramento and two in San Francisco. This was an attempt to keep the family together. We still had a residency in Harrisburg.

Then in 2004, we bought a 1774 farmhouse in Palmyra, Pennsylvania, a four-and-a-half acre homesite within the town limits. The house had good bones but had not been lived in for at least seven years. We turned the house into a beautiful historic park. The property had approximately 120 trees, which we cut down to about forty-five—making the property manageable. We spent seven years between Tahoe and Palmyra. It was a beautiful stone-built five-thousand-square-foot farmhouse with an old corn barn as an outbuilding. We sold this house in 2001, another seven years in my life.

We went on and rented an apartment in Durham, North Carolina, to help my oldest son, Brian, as he was going through his residency in emergency medicine at Duke University School of Medicine. Upon Brian finishing his residency in 2013, we moved to Reno, Nevada, selling our Tahoe house and preparing to build our own home there. We purchased a lot and planned to build on it. As I was a contractor my whole life, I took on the supervision of the work. We built a six-thousand-square-foot timber frame home with a view of the Sierra Nevada about twenty-five miles from Truckee, California, which was twelve miles north of Tahoe. We lived in the house for three years, a total of five years in Reno—two years while building and three years in our new home. A total of seventeen years on the West Coast—twelve in Tahoe and five in Reno.

We then relocated to northeast Georgia, where we are today. From the time I got remarried, I felt like I was on a quest for God's purpose for me. I learned that on my birthday, day became night from 12:00 p.m. to 3:00 p.m. (sixth to ninth hour). I felt like it matched the scripture in his description of Matthew 24:29, but I did not notice it at the time as it was precisely that verse. It was because of the word *immediately* as the first word of the verse.

The things that happen in my life are associated with specific numbers. The number seven that I've gone over in my description of my life. The number thirteen shows up on the dates of my mother's birth, my birth, and my father's death. The number seventeen is probably the most profound number. I talked about having eighteen years of service with both my wife and Heim Electric. Twenty-four is also one.

Let's go over these numbers:

- 7: I was conceived on my parents' seventh wedding anniversary, December 26, 1949.

    o When I was seven years old, we moved from Lock Haven to Hummelstown in 1957.
    o I was in business for seven years, then retired.
    o We owned a 1774 farmhouse for seven years and sold it (from 2004 to 2011). Also, the barn that I purchased in 1997 and sold, I believe, in 2004, was also seven years.

- 13: My mother's birthday is June 13, 1920.

  - My father died on December 13, 1986.
  - September 24, 1950, my birthday, is also Tishri 13, Black Sunday.

- 17: My brother, Richard, the oldest of three boys, was killed in a car accident on August 17, 1960.

  - My brother Larry Dayne died at the age of seventy on January 17, 2017.
  - I was seventeen when I was nicknamed Noah.
  - I was married for the first time on May 17, 1975.
  - Pat and I lived on the West Coast—in Tahoe for twelve years and Reno for five years—for a total of seventeen years.
  - Pat found the house that we have now in Hiawassee, Georgia, and the seventeen-mile marker is right beside our driveway.
  - My two brothers and I all have seventeen letters in our names: Richard Lee Burrows, Larry Dayne Burrows, and Thomas Lynn Burrows.

- 18: The Monday before Easter 1993, I separated from my wife.

  - On the Monday before Easter 1994, I was terminated from my work with the Edwin L. Heim Company.
  - I had eighteen years of service with each. Eighteen has the meaning of freedom from bondage.

- 24: I was born on September 24, 1950, also called Tishri 13, or Black Sunday.

  - My oldest brother, Richard, was born on August 24, 1945.

- ○ The last two numbers on my Social Security number are twenty-four.
- ○ I was twenty-four when I got married.
- ○ My father was twenty-four when my parents got married.
- ○ In my second marriage, I was forty-eight, or two times twenty-four.

These interesting facts kept me looking further into what the Holy Spirit was telling me. In my studies of the events of my birthday, I found a tetrad. I have a whole section on tetrads—tetrad from 1949–1950, with September 25, 1950, being the day of the last eclipse of this tetrad. September 26 was the first day of the Feast of Tabernacles, September 24–26. In Matthew 24:15, Jesus speaks of Daniel's prophecy of the abomination of desolation. That prophecy is in chapter 9 (September), verses 24–27. Matching the dates of events except for 9:27 fulfills all of these verses, but in 2014 and 2015, a tetrad where the last lunar eclipse was on 9:27 fulfilled all four verses. I call this Donald Trump's tetrad, which is significant because the Lord has His hand on Donald Trump to become the president of the United States, which he became on January 20, 2017.

My name, Thomas, and the disciple Thomas was not a doubter but merely needed confirmation. I, too, am a seeker of confirmation, also with regard to the nickname Noah. My name, Thomas, in Hebrew, means twin with myself, being born on the day that's the beginning of the generation and being given this knowledge that we are in the beginning of the world being transformed into what God has shown us in Revelation.

We moved to Georgia in November 2018, found a house, and settled on February 28. Upon moving to Georgia, we needed a new driver's license and license plates for our car. Upon buying a new 2019 Lexus RX 350, we received the license plate off the top of the pile. There was no special plate; this one said CAM 1950. This was indeed a confirmation from God that I was looking for. 1950 is the year of the generation, and with advanced study, the word *cam* is Greek for go boldly. It was the word used in the gospels describing

Joseph of Arimathea as he went *boldly* to Pilate. I was looking for this confirmation, and God provided it: the parable of the fig tree, Black Sunday, the tetrad, a solar eclipse on Rosh Hashanah in 1950, and the dates matching Daniel's prophecy.

I believe I'm being told to tell the world this boldly. After Pat and I had been married for several years, I read about the heritage of my wife's deceased husband and their family. They were of German descent, with the last name Balsbaugh or Balsbach in Germany. They settled in the Hummelstown/Hershey area in the early 1700s. My family moved there in 1957. Settling on the farm of the farmer called Grandpa Saufley. Grandpa had a son, Alva, who bought another farm approximately four miles from Grandpa Saufley's farm. Thomas's brother, Ed, wrote a lineage study of his ancestry. This is where I found some of this. And it just so happens that Thomas's great-great-grandfather, one of the early 1700 residents of that area, is buried on Alva Saufley's farm.

There was a church between the two farms, now called the Hanoverdale Brethren Church. It had previously been a Dunkard Church, of which Valentine Balsbaugh was the pastor. In the cemetery of Hanoverdale Church, there are at least half a dozen Balsbaugh headstones where Thomas's ancestors are buried; they were among the first people buried in that cemetery. Valentine passed away in the later part of the 1700s. This cemetery probably wasn't constructed when he got buried on Alva's farm. My brother, who passed away before my father and mother in 1960, is buried in that same cemetery. At the time, my father purchased four burial lots there. My mother and father are also buried there. Interestingly, Pat's first husband, G. Thomas Balsbaugh, was the third son of three boys. His father was the second son of three boys. I am the third son of three boys, and my father is the second son of three boys—each of us with the name Thomas. God's hand is upon many of us. He's been steadfast with me since conception. I've done an interesting study that I call the third born. I'll put that together in another chapter that shows a parallel between Abraham's family and mine. God works in patterns. Is my life a pattern of one that's already happened? Time will be the teller.

Study of the Third Born

We will study Genesis and Exodus to see this fantastic line of chosen lineage. God protected chosen sons, marrying their sisters and nieces to keep a protected DNA line. Adam knew Eve and conceived Cain and Abel. They had sinned before this, and we will see sin taking over humans' DNA. Cain killing his brother, Abel, makes us aware of this fact. Cain being banished, who has married one of his sisters. There were no other humans on earth other than Adam and Eve's children. Then when Adam was 130 years old, Eve bore Seth, the third-born son. Seth's line carried the chosen line through Enoch, the seventh born from Adam. Methuselah, the eighth from Adam, lived to be the oldest human ever at 969 years old and the only pre-flood patriarch whose age was divisible by seventeen, a number that indicates victory. His grandson, Noah, was the tenth from Adam. Noah had three sons: Shem, Ham, and Japheth. Japheth, the eldest, and Shem, the third born. The children of Shem are Elam, Asshur, Arphaxad, Lud, and Aram. Notice the order of Noah's sons, from youngest to eldest. I believe this is true of Shem's sons, with Arphaxad being the third born and the son carrying on the chosen lineage. The Arphaxad line goes on to Terah, the father of Abram, who had three sons: Abram, Nahor, and Haran. Haran, the eldest, and Abram, the youngest— the third born. Haran was born when Terah was seventy years old, and Abram was born when Terah was 130 years old, the same age Adam was when he had Seth. So Abram was sixty years younger than Haran. Haran had a son, Lot, a daughter, Milcah, and a daughter, Iscah. Iscah is believed to be Sarai, Abrams' wife. Haran died before his father. His brother Nahor married his brother's daughter, his niece. Abram also married his brother's daughter and his niece. Interestingly, all family members except Lot and Milcah had five letters in their names. Five has the meaning of grace. After Tarah died at 205 years old, Abram was told by God to leave and go to Cannan, the promised land, which was given to the Jewish people. Abram was seventy-five years old.

Abram took Lot and his wife, Sarai, with him. Sarai was barren, but God had promised Abram that his seed would grow into nations. Sarai was not patient and gave Abram her handmaiden Hagar as a wife, and she conceived and had Ishmael, creating conflict between Sarah and Hagar. Hagar left with Ishmael, but God instructed her to return; Sarai, who then became Sarah, conceived at eighty-nine. She had Isaac, her son, at the age of ninety. Abram became Abraham, who was a hundred years old when Isaac was born. Both name changes are an example of being born again. So Abram had two sons in his first family. After Isaac was born, there was additional trouble between Hagar and Sarah, so God instructed Hagar and Ishmael to leave and promised to bless them both. Ishmael, the oldest, and Isaac, the second born.

Isaac needed a wife, and Abram sent his servant, Eleisner, to fetch a wife for Isaac. He went to his brother's descendants and found Rebekah, the granddaughter of Milcah and Nahor. Eleisner brought back Rebekah as a wife for Isaac. Isaac and Rebekah knew each other and conceived twins, Esau and Jacob. Esau came out first, and Jacob's hand was on Esau's heel. Esau, being the firstborn, deserved the firstborn's blessing but felt little need for it. He was an accomplished hunter, very proud of himself. He felt he did not need it. He sold his blessing for a bowl of soup to Isaac. Then Rebekah and Jacob fooled Isaac into receiving the blessing from his father. Esau was angry, and Jacob was worried that Esau would kill him. Rebekah then sent him off to her brother Laban, where Jacob married two of his daughters, who would have been his cousins. Jacob's first wife, Leah, was fertile. His second wife, Rachel, was barren. In this order, Leah had four sons: Reuben, Simon, Levi, and Judah. The Bible shows us this order specifically. These were the first four sons of Jacob, who had twelve sons and one daughter with two wives and two maidservants. Notice that the third-born son was Levi. Levi's descendants became the priesthood. Levi's daughter married her nephew, and the offspring were Moses's parents. Both parents were Levites, and Moses was the third born from them. Moses then had two sons. The Levite lineage ran true to Christ's time in that Zacharias and Elizabeth, the parents of John the Baptist, were both Levites, making John the Baptist a priest and firstborn.

Looking back at Terah's family, who was the father of Abram, I see similarities uncannily with my family. These were the points of interest. Abraham was the third-born son. I was the third-born son. Abrams's older brother, Haron, died before his father. My oldest brother, Richard, died before my father. All of Abram and his brothers have five letters in their names. All my brothers and I have seventeen letters in our names—seventeen have the meaning of victory—Richard Lee Burrows, Larry Dayne Burrows, and Thomas Lynn Burrows. Abraham had two sons in his first family. I had two sons in my first family. Hagar and Ishmael were sent away without contact with Abram. I sent my first wife away by divorce. My oldest is just like Ishmael in that he has taken himself away. He is an emergency medical doctor at Duke Regional Hospital and is absent from my wife and my life. He has three boys and a daughter, the daughter of whom I've never seen, and he has eliminated himself from our family. As you see, my life has many interesting items that I believe God has His hand on. These facts confirm that my purpose is to inform the world about *the beginning of the transformation to eternal life*. This the reason I am writing this book.

Donald Trump has recently been shown to have had divine intervention by God. This encouraged me to study a few things, as I have indicated before that the 2014–2015 tetrad was a Donald Trump tetrad. He is definitely chosen by God for God's timing. Interestingly, God has given Donald this wealth to ward off these attacks. He also seems to have a heart like God's and King David's, as a product of divine intervention. Looking back at his life, Donald's older brother died before his father. Donald showed how evil the political system is—not only the whole Democratic Party but half of the Republican Party as well. God's hand showed on July 13, 2024. That divine intervention prevented Donald from being assassinated by an assassin's bullet.

Donald and I have this in common: we are here for the will and purpose of being Christ's servants, asking God for His will every day. This book shows the world that!

The Chosen

Shining the light on evil or outing evil. Looking back at Scripture, God has a good track record of doing this. Generally, He raises a chosen man for the job. Moses was one of the first men to do this job. Joseph, son of Jacob, or Israel, had saved Egypt from famine by following God's guidance. Pharaoh recognized Joseph's gift of being a "chosen one" of God. A new evil pharaoh took over Egypt and didn't care about Joseph or his God. God chose Moses to show how evil Pharaoh was. God had Moses confront Pharaoh and command, "Let the Jewish people go," but Pharaoh was stubborn and refused. God put eleven plagues on Egypt. Most scholars claim ten but forget God's collapse in the Red Sea as the last plague. Confronting Pharaoh's evilness brought anger from Pharaoh, even at the time his oldest son died. This whole story was completed for one thing and one thing only, and that's God's Glory.

The next chosen was David, the king of Israel. As a young man, he slew Goliath, a symbol of pride and arrogance against God's people. He raised David, creating him with a heart like God's. David's line would bring on the Messiah.

Yeshua, the Savior, Jesus Christ, the Messiah, came to save the world from the world's problem: sin. He outed the evil Pharisees, which angered them. He did this to accomplish His mission to be killed and then rise again on the third day.

The Catholic Church of today was created by Constantinople, which gave the church a role and authority over the people. They were placed with absolute power in the government. Power corrupts, and absolute power absolutely corrupts. God then tolerated this for many years as they misinterpreted the Scripture. Many Nicolaitans in church leadership positions control people with deceit and false interpretation.

Then in the late 1400s, God brought a man called Martin Luther, and in the first half of the 1500s, Martin outed the church for its controlling methods called indulgences. When he posted his ninety-five theses on the Wittenberg door in 1517, it sent shockwaves through the Catholic Church. And as they had done in the past, they sought to kill Martin. God protected him through Prince Fredrick, the owner of the Wittenberg Seminary. It's in Wittenberg where Martin translated the Torah and the New Testament into German for the German people to read for themselves. The tearing of the veil of the holy of holies when Christ was crucified was God's signal that he was available to all who sought Him directly. No priest was needed. The Reformation period presented a departure from religious persecution in Europe to go to the New World, America. Ironically, Martin has three tetrads that identify specific things that he has done. You can find that in the chapter on the tetrads.

The Jews were given the land of the Canaanites as the promised land, which was given to Abraham and his descendants. America is a parallel to the promised land of the Jews. The Jews are the bride of the Father. The church, a body of believers headed by Christ, is the bride of Christ. This church is not the Catholic Church, although there are members of the body who are also members of the Catholic Church. America is the land of plenty for the bride of Christ.

In the late 1700s, when America was England's colony, God raised His chosen to form a country with a constitution that allowed freedom of religion and freedom of the people. The chosen consisted of George Washington, John Adams, Thomas Jefferson, and other leaders, but many followed them to form a perfect union for freedom.

Trouble arose in the mid-1800s when, as America was arguing the slavery issue, the adversary, Satan, raised his man Darwin. That brought out his thesis in 1859, making the white European at the top of the human order. The Black and Asian races were the link between white men and the apes. This was liked by the Democrat southern slave owners. This gave them scientific evidence, although false, to treat the imprisoned enslaved people below human treatment. People today say Darwin had a bias or bigotry in his thesis. I say he made an obvious mistake. That could not have continued with today's trends.

Darwin made many mistakes in his theories that some evolutionary scientists refuse to acknowledge as part of God's creation.

Abraham Lincoln was chosen for this outing of evil. He became our president to help guide us through this difficulty. The South was slow to change but significantly transformed from those days of segregation. The adversary, Satan, wasn't going to give up easily. He created the KKK and the Jim Crow laws, all of the doing of southern Democrats. The same evil southern Democratic Party that refuses to give up control of its people. The Democratic Party found a way to keep control of its voting population. The Blacks were poor and grouped into cities, and the Democrats gained control of the city government. Poor education methods and the flooding of drug trafficking into these cities kept these people under a form of slavery. The government would use taxpayer money to buy votes from this population.

Today, there are two men in a race for our presidency. One is chosen by God, Yahweh, and the other is chosen by the adversary, Satan. Donald Trump has a tetrad that shows his earmark. In 2014 and 2015, he was God's pick to raise and show the evilness of the Democratic Party, and they showed how evil they were. They weren't and are not shy about showing how evil they are. Joe Biden was born in Scranton, Pennsylvania, then moved to Delaware and became a senator. This man has lied, stolen, and sold out America for his gain. He is and was a bigot. He doesn't have any boundaries. Saturday, July 13, 2024, someone tried to assassinate Donald Trump. God protected His chosen.

Joe Biden is now politically forced to slow down his evil, false rhetoric. Donald Trump is a chosen man who was brought up and blessed with much wealth so he could fight this fight. People don't see this, but this is all about God's glory and His man, Donald Trump. God showed us on Saturday by having Donald move his head just at the right moment to avoid that bullet. The adversary is busy, for he knows his time is short. God is setting all this up for the end of the ages. We set back, anticipating what would come next. But God, knowing what will happen, has promised His own eternal life with Him and His promise to His Church, the body of believers that He is the head of. There is no need to worry if you are part of that body. It's better you never lived if you are not. And if you are or have become a born-again Christian, having the Holy Spirit in your heart is a great assurance. There is nothing on this earth that should worry you. God is in control, and His promises to us are eternal life, where there is no evil. For like darkness has no substance, God is the light of the world. Evil does not exist in that eternal world, as light from God eliminates its existence.

One more chosen person, and that's me, Thomas Lynn Burrows—not bragging, just acknowledging that through all things God has shown me through my life and being born on the day that was the beginning of the end of the ages, showing me His signs, His wonders to His chosen. We are in the winter (last season) of the generation. Jesus spoke up in Matthew 24:34; Mark 13:30; and Luke 21:30 to read the chapters of my life to further understand. This is entirely for *God's glory*, nothing else. Jesus plus nothing equals everything.

The Amazing Tabernacle

Let's look at what Scripture says about this amazing structure. This is Exodus 25:1–9:

> Then the Lord spoke to Moses, saying: "Speak to the children of Israel, that they bring Me an offering. From everyone who gives it willingly with his heart you shall take My offering. And this is the offering which you shall take from them: gold, silver, and bronze; blue, purple, and scarlet thread, fine linen, and goats' hair; ram skins dyed red, badger skins, and acacia/shittim wood; oil for the light, and spices for the anointing oil and for the sweet incense; onyx stones, and stones to be set in the ephod and in the breastplate. And let them make Me a sanctuary, that I may dwell among them. According to all that I show you, that is, the pattern of the tabernacle and the pattern of all its furnishings, just so you shall make it."

We see here that God is speaking to Moses, so God is instructing this to be built. Specific materials are needed, and all these materials have biblical meanings. This is necessary to understand the significance of the tabernacle.

Item	Biblical Meaning	References
• gold	deity	1 Corinthians 3:12; Revelation 21:18–21

- silver   redemption   Exodus 36:24; 30:15
- bronze   judgment   Exodus 27:2; Numbers 21:9; Revelation 1:15
- blue   heavens/heavenly   Exodus 25:4; 26:31; 28:31
- purple   kingship/royalty   John 19:2; Revelation 17:4
- scarlet   blood sacrifice   Leviticus 14:4; Joshua 2:18; Isaiah 1:18
- fine linen   righteousness   Leviticus 6:10; Revelation 9:8
- goat's hair   atonement   Genesis 15:9; Exodus 12:5
- acacia wood   humanity   Exodus 26:15; Isaiah 53:2
- oil   Holy Spirit   Leviticus 14:16; Psalm 47:7

As we study the construction, it's crucial to keep in mind the depth of these materials. They reveal what God had planned to show us about the future ages and the specific meanings and time periods. This structure holds profound truths. This study will be an engaging journey for investigative reporters and puzzle enthusiasts, putting many pieces of the puzzle in place.

> The length of the court shall be a hundred cubits,
> and the breadth fifty everywhere, and the height
> five cubits of fine twined linen, and their sockets
> of brass. (Exodus 27:18)

The outer court

So the outer court's curtain is three hundred cubits in total length by five cubits high in size, making this curtain 1500 square cubits in area; the curtain was blue, purple, and scarlet thread. The blue-purple would make you think you're entering a heavenly place of royalty. Scarlet reminds you that this is a place of sacrifice and blood. This place has the feeling of righteousness. As you pass through the gate, you will see the brass altar with its perpetual fire.

And thou shalt make an altar of acacia/ shittim wood, five cubits long, and five cubits broad; the altar shall be foursquare: and the height thereof shall be three cubits. And thou shalt make the horns of it upon the four corners thereof: his horns shall be of the same: and thou shalt overlay it with brass. And thou shalt make his pans to receive his ashes, and his shovels, and his basons, and his flesh hooks, and his firepans: all the vessels thereof thou shalt make of brass. And thou shalt make for it a grate of network of brass; and upon the net shalt thou make four brasen rings in the four corners thereof. And thou shalt put it under the compass of the altar beneath, that the net may be even to the midst of the altar. And thou shalt make staves for the altar, staves of shittim wood, and overlay them with brass. And the staves shall be put into the rings, and the staves shall be upon the two sides of the altar, to bear it. Hollow with boards shalt thou make it: as it was shewed thee in the mount, so shall they make it. (Exodus 27:1–8)

As you can see, all the furniture and utensils in the outer court were made of brass. As you enter the gate, the altar is set right in front of you with four horns, one in each corner of the altar, to tie down the unwilling sacrifice. It's apparent this area speaks of judgment and law; the fire is perpetual, and so are the sacrifices and the shedding of blood.

The cross eliminated the need for the altar and the continual sacrifice. No horns were needed. As Christ went willingly to the cross saying, Greater love has no one than this, that he lay down his life for his friends. Also, the fires of God's judgment, burn out in Christ's crucifixion and resurrection, and those who are now baptized by the Spirit or in Christ are forever safe. God's fire of judgment still exists and will be exercised in the Tribulation period and the great white throne. Everyone who does not believe in the Son, Christ, paid the debt for sin, which is taken care of through the blood of Christ. Those who reject His gift of salvation must pay the price of sin. Between the altar and the tent, take a closer look at the inner chamber and holy of holies. We see a bronze laver that the priests were instructed to wash thoroughly before entering the inner chamber or holy place. The laver is made of brass and was used as a mirror to see yourself and the sinful man you are, in need of a Savior: the Messiah, Jesus Christ. Also, the law was intended for that purpose, so one could see how imperfect they are compared to the law. Seeing our flaws and the need for redemption of sin.

The inner chamber or holy place

The holy place, after the labor and through washing, the priest could enter the sacred place, which was a section of the enclosure. The size of the holy place is ten cubits wide, twenty cubits deep, and ten cubits high. With some math, we find it to be two thousand cubic cubits—some amazing furniture in the holy place. First, we will look at the showbread table. Its construction is of acacia wood or smitten wood, two cubits by one cubit by one and a half cubits high. It shall be overlaid with a pure gold roundabout. Then a hand breathed around, and a golden crown surrounded the border. All the utensils, dishes, spoons, covers, and bowls shall be pure gold. Showbread shall be on the table constantly.

This is an amazing illustration of our Savior, the Messiah, Jesus Christ. The wood symbolizes Christ's humanity. The gold overlay would be Christ's deity. The crown around about signifies His kingship. Christ as the bread of life, with this being the showbread table.

The altar of incense is again a piece of furniture made of acacia or smitten wood, overlaid in gold. Aaron's Levites must burn fragrant incense on the altar each morning while tending the lamps and at dusk or twilight. So incense will burn regularly for generations in the future. The essence of Jesus Christ is our prayerful connection, or intercessory, to the Father. The incense is an example of our prayers lifted up to Christ, who delivers them to the Father. It is to be revered as holy, the same way Christ is holy and cannot be substituted. There is only one intercessory, and that's Christ Himself.

The amazing lamp, the menorah

The golden lamp was meticulously crafted from a single piece of gold, starting with a single large piece that couldn't have any gold added once the crafting process began. It consists of seven lamps—one center lamp and three on each side of the center. Each of the six side lamps is adorned with almond bowls, knobs, and flowers, with three of each on all six side lamps. The center lamp features four almond bowls, knobs, and flowers. The side lamps have a total of nine almond items each, and the center lamp has a total of twelve. When you total the almond items, including the three side lamps and the center lamp, you get thirty-nine—the same number of books in the Old Testament of the English Bible. The remaining three side lamps, with nine almond items each, total twenty-seven—the same number of books in the New Testament. Total of sixty-six in the New and Old Testaments.

The significance of the lamp being hammered from a single piece of gold is that it symbolizes the Word, or the Bible. Just as Christ is the light of the world, the Bible also serves as a guiding light. The fact that the lamp was formed from one piece of gold signifies that the Holy Spirit had a hand in all sixty-six books. This information about the tabernacle, written by Moses around 1450 BC, foreshadows things to come about Christ, the Bible, and His redeeming love for us—where He selflessly gave Himself to die for the forgiveness of our sins. It is a remarkable demonstration of love.

Holy of holies

This is the last part of the tent enclosure. It measures ten cubits wide, ten cubits deep, and ten cubits high, making a total of one thousand cubic cubits. A veil separates the holy place from the holy of holies, which only the high priest can enter, and only once a year on Yom Kippur, the tenth of the month of Tishrei, which generally falls in September or October. The veil is no ordinary one, as it is made of twisted linen of blue, purple, and scarlet and is reported to be four inches thick. When Christ died on the cross at the ninth hour of Nisan 14, AD 30, the veil in the temple was torn from top to bottom, which was an act of the Father. This event signified that the holy of holies was open to all, not just the high priest. Inside the holy of holies, we find the ark of the covenant, a box made of acacia wood with two golden boxes, one inside and one outside, representing the Trinity, humanity, and deity. The ark also has a covering called the mercy seat, where God was present with the high priest on Yom Kippur. The ark of the covenant contains a golden jar holding manna, Aaron's rod, which budded, and the tablets containing the Ten Commandments. The manna symbolizes the perfect food for the wilderness; Aaron's rod signifies God's miraculous power in producing fruit from a dead rod and the tablets of stone with the Ten Commandments were written by God's finger. This shows the materials used and their biblical meanings.

The tabernacle had three sections, each with its own dimensions and significance. Solomon's temple replaced the tabernacle and was destroyed in 586 BC by Nebuchadnezzar, the king of Babylon. Herod the Great later built a new temple, which was destroyed by the Roman General Titus in AD 70. Christ was crucified on April 5, AD 30, and there were temple sacrifices both before and after his crucifixion. The veil in the temple tore at the ninth hour when Christ died, but the Jews may not have understood its significance and may have repaired it. During Yom Kippur, two goats were chosen, one to be sacrificed and one as the scapegoat. A lot was drawn from a black or white ball to make the choice. From AD 30 to AD 70, only a black ball was drawn when making the choice, which goes against mathematical probability. God tried to show the Jews that there was a significant change. Prior to AD 30, a scarlet cord tied to the temple door would turn white the next day, indicating forgiveness of sins for that year. However, after AD 30, the cord would not turn white; it remained red, indicating that forgiveness of sins now came from believing in Jesus Christ as your Savior and not from temple sacrifices.

The study of the tabernacle should be a required topic in every Christian church to demonstrate the love and glory of our great Lord Jesus, the Messiah. All praise, glory, and honor to Him.

- three distinct areas of the tabernacle
- three dispensational periods
- three time periods for each
- how they match salvation

Area	Dispensational Period	Volume	Aspect of Salvation
The outer court	Law Period	1,500 SW cubits	Justification
	Mosaic Law	1,500 (years)	
The inner chamber	Period of Grace	2,000 cubic cubits	Sanctification
	The Church Age	2,000 (years)	
The holy of holies	Millennium Period	1,000 cubic cubits	Glorification
		1,000 (years)	

AD 30, the year Christ was crucified, plus two thousand years (inner chamber) is 2030/2031

The start of generation 1950, plus the length of seventy–eighty years is 2030/2031

Jesus's Crucifixion year AD 30 was four thousand years from Adam's sin plus two thousand years to make six thousand is 2030/2031 for the Messiah to return for the Jews at year 6000.

No day or time mentioned but three ways show the same on or before time.

The Jewish Calendar 5784

The year is an error with scripture when sized up with the Tanakh. Archbishop James Ussher completed a study of the Tanakh to establish the beginning of creation. His study is in *The Annals of the World*. He started with the historically known year of the temple's destruction in 586/587 BC and went backward toward Adam. Rosh Hashanah on Tishri 1, 2 begins the Jewish year and marks the day creation started. James puts that day in 4005 BC as the Sunday after the fall equinox. He has listed the dates of every biblical event, taking us back to the beginning of creation in 4005 BC or 4004 years to AD 1—no zero year, so 1 BC and AD 1 are the same year. So in calculation, you must subtract a year from BC years to get the number of years from a BC date. In his study, he compared the *Seder Olam Rabbah* with the Tanakh. The *Seder Olam Rabbah* is a Jewish writing detailing the dates of biblical events from creation to Alexander the Great's conquest of Persia and is the tool used for the Jewish calendar of the year 5784.

James Ussher discovered a few errors made by the Jewish rabbis in their calculations. There were four errors at the time. The first was Abram's birth. The Jewish Seder has Abraham born 1,948 years from creation, the fact is that it was 2,008 years from creation. They had Terah as seventy years old at Abram's birth, when the Tanakh showed Terah as 130 years old when Abram was born—a sixty-year shortcoming. The Seder Olam listed five hundred years from Abram's birth to the Exodus. In reality, it was 505 years, a five-year shortcoming. The Seder Olam and Ussher reckoning were the same from the Exodus to the laying of the foundation of the temple—zero years difference. The difference between the foundation of the first temple and the construction of the second temple Usher is 497 years, from 1012 BC to 515 BC. The Seder Olam listed 480 years, from 831 to 351 BC, a seventeen-year shortfall. Then from the consecration of the second temple to its destruction by Titus of Rome, Ussher 584 years (575 BC to AD 70) and the Seder Olam 420 years (351 BC to AD 70)—a shortfall of 164 years. Sixty plus five plus seventeen plus 164 equals a 246-year shortfall. We added 5784 and got our calendar year from the creation of 6030, knowing Ussher has 4004 years calculated from creation to AD 1/1 BC, plus the year 2024 would be 6028. Knowing each error calculation could be half a year off makes Ussher's master number of 4004 years from creation more accurate. This also lines up Christ being born four thousand years from Adam's creation and four meaning the world and Christ came to save the world.

The correct Jewish year for 2024/2025. Jews believe the Messiah will come in their calendar year six thousand from creation. Their starting point is off because Adam and Eve would have lived forever if nobody had sinned. Sin is the starting point, and that's unknown. We do know Adam and Eve sinned before having Cain and Abel. We can get a window into that by assuming a few things. Cain and Abel seemed to be young adults of, I guess, more than twenty years. That would take more than twenty years after they sinned, and they must have had daughters for Cain to marry—no other humans. Then Seth was born when Adam was 130 years old.

It is my belief that Jesus was born in the four thousandth year of creation, in September of 5 BC, and that Christ was crucified in AD 30, which was four thousand years from Adam's sin—a belief not confirmed by scripture. However, it is possible to interpret 2030 or 2031 as the six thousandth year of Adam and Eve's sin. This interpretation aligns with the generation starting in September 1950 and adding eighty to eighty-one years (Psalm 90:10) for the length of that generation, leading to the conclusion of 2030 or 2031 for Christ's return. The Jewish calendar correctly shows us the period from 2030 to 2031, a period that holds significant potential.

Always be aware that no man knows the day or hour, but 1 Thessalonians chapter 5 tells us we should be aware of the season as we are of light and not of darkness. We are definitely in the *winter* of the generation to see the Rapture and those left behind to see the Tribulation period.

Another perspective is the tabernacle; the size of the inner chamber or holy place is two thousand cubic cubits. The holy of holies is one thousand cubic cubits, symbolizing the millennium of one thousand years. The outer chamber has a curtain around it of 1,500 square cubits with bronze items, with bronze having the biblical meaning of the law or the period of the law. When Moses received the law, Christ fulfilled the law. This connection between the tabernacle and biblical time frames serves to enlighten and connect us to the historical and spiritual significance of these events.

Historians have Moses receiving the law between 1491 BC and 1450 BC. If it were 1471 BC plus AD 30 for Christ's fulfillment of the law, that would be 1,500 years the same size as the curtain—three hundred cubits long by five cubits high or 1,500 square cubits. Then the inner chamber has the shewbread table, the menorah lamp, and all things that point to Christ or the period of grace where Christ's bride is gathered. The inner chamber is two thousand cubic cubits—AD 30, the start of the age of grace, plus two thousand years is 2030 or 2031. I'm not trying to date, but to show three biblical ways, 2030/2031 is the result.

How amazing is our *Lord?*

Study of Jesus's Birth and Death Dates

When studying Scripture, one must be concise and detailed about the truth. It's like putting a puzzle together with Scripture and history to get the right piece in the right place. A misplaced piece will hinder future pieces from being placed correctly. All scripture is accurate. If your interpretation of scripture conflicts with other scripture, your interpretation is wrong. Hence, if a piece of the puzzle is incorrect, it will hinder the proper placement of future studies to be accurate. These incorrect puzzle pieces have been placed in the past and present, some intentionally and some unintentionally. To start a study of Jesus's birth, death, and resurrection, we need to look at Scripture thoroughly. Each of the four gospels gives a different view of Christ's life.

Matthew tells the story of the wise men. Josephus tells us that Herod the Great died a terrible death in the spring of 4 BC. Knowing this tells us Jesus needed to be born before this for Matthew's story to be true. Luke tells us that in the fifteenth year of the reign of Caesar Tiberius, the Word of God came to the son of Zacharias in the wilderness, or John the Baptist (Luke 3:1–2). Jesus is baptized, and verse 23 states that Jesus Himself began to be about thirty years old. So all these things have to match. Studying Tiberius, we find that Augustus died on August of AD 14. Then Tiberius was made Caesar. With AD 14 being the start year of Tiberius's reign, AD 28 or 29 is the fifteenth year of his reign. Subtracting thirty years puts Christ's birth at 1 or 2 BC. This does not work with Herod the Great's death. So in relooking at history, we find Augustus made Tiberius *co-Caesar* in AD 12, making AD 12 Tiberius's starting point. Then with this new info, Tiberius's fifteenth year of reign is AD 26 or 27. Subtracting thirty years from Jesus's age puts Jesus's birth year at 5 BC. This works with all scripture and verified history.

Now let's look at the time of year Jesus was born. In a study of Zacharias, who was John the Baptist's father, we find he was servicing the temple when an angel met with him, telling him that his wife, Elizabeth, would give birth to a son. Zacharias was hesitant to believe this, as he and Elizabeth were old and she had been barren. The angel made Zacharias mute for his unbelief. Zacharias was in the eighth group of Levites to serve the temple. The rotation would start on Nisan 1, with each group serving a week, and all groups would help during festivals, which put Zacharias in the temple at the end of May or beginning of June, making June the month Zacharias went home and conceived John the Baptist. The Scripture noted that Elizebeth hid her pregnancy for five months. In her sixth month of pregnancy, Mary was just impregnated by the Holy Spirit with Jesus in her womb and visited Elizabeth, which makes December the month they met. Adding three more months for Elizabeth to give birth to John the Baptist puts John's birth in March or April. Adding nine months to Mary's conception, the month of December puts Christ's birth in September. John's birth date per the Jewish calendar would be Nisan, and Christ's birth would be in the Jewish calendar month of Tishri. So Christ was born in September of 5 BC. John's birth was around or on the Festival of Passover. Jesus Christ's birth would be around the high holy days of Rosh Hashanah, Yom Kippur, and the Feast of Tabernacles. A 5 BC birth of Christ puts Christ's birth at four thousand years from creation. Four has the biblical meaning the world, and Christ came to save it.

Look at Jesus's teaching years as the Gospel of John, the best chronological time frame. The fifteenth year of Tiberius was from the fall of AD 26 to the fall of AD 27. Another prophecy in Daniel guides us on when this baptism occurred. Interestingly, this prophecy is the 483 years of the 490-year prophecy in Daniel 9:24–26, with 9/27 being the last seven years of the 490-year prophecy. A known date in Ezra is when the king of Persia permitted the Jews to rebuild their city, Jerusalem. This was in 458 BC, which would be 457 years to AD 1. Four hundred fifty-seven plus AD 26 makes 483 years, fulfilling this prophecy at the baptism of Christ, confirming AD 26. Jesus taught and preached through three Passovers and was crucified on the fourth Passover after His baptism. This puts Christ's crucifixion in the year AD 30. Now look at AD 30 to see if Nisan 14 lines up as it should. Different Jewish calendars were listed then, but confirmation could be established from NASA's full moon and new moon lists. The fifteenth of the month of the Jewish calendar is generally the full moon. In AD 30, NASA's full moon fell on April 6, a Thursday, which would have been Nisan 15. Jesus was crucified on Nisan 14, or preparation day for Passover. Nisan 15 is the first day of the festival of unleavened bread, a Sabbath. The fifteenth through the twenty-first are a seven-day festival.

The 14th of Nisan in AD 30 was on a Wednesday, not a Friday. This confirms that Good Friday is the wrong piece in the puzzle. Matthew 12:40 tells us, "For as Jonah was three days and three nights in the whale's belly; so shall the Son of Man be three days and three nights in the heart of the earth."

Remember, if Scripture shows you wrong, you are wrong; get over it. Good Friday is in error, either on purpose or not; it doesn't matter because it hides God's *glory*. His glory is shown by the calendar days He was crucified on Nisan 14, also April 5, was the day Christ was crucified. Fourteen means salvation, and five means grace. Jesus Christ died to save us by grace. He rose after being in the heart of the earth for three nights and three days. Jesus Christ rose from the dead on the eve of Nisan 17, also April 8. Seventeen, biblically means victory, and eight means a new beginning. Jesus was victorious over death and fulfilled the law, creating a new beginning, the start of the church age, the age of grace. To add to that, 30, the year, means the blood of Jesus Christ. This is *God's glory*, do not hide it.

He shows us His glory by the dates He was crucified and rose, but wait, He was found risen on the first day of the week, Sunday, before daylight. That day was Nisan 18 and April 9. Eighteen biblically means the freedom of bondage, and nine represents the fruits of the Spirit or Holy Spirit. He was free of the bondage of death and would leave and bring us the Holy Spirit, whose job it is to find the bride of Christ, the church, and the body of believers with Christ to become our husband.

The Catholic Church, which has shown in its past to be very anti-Semitic, has not adhered to Scripture showing the Jewish calendar as the method to locate the festivals per the Jewish calendar. The Catholic Church started around AD 330, when Constantinople made Christianity part of the Roman government. Power corrupts, and absolute power corrupts. So now we have the correct puzzle piece that will allow more pieces to be placed. The refusal of pastors and theologians to ignore the proper pieces is an effort by Satan to hide God's glory. Throughout history, Satan has been very active in this. Today, I hear theologians and historians saying that the Bible is not a history book but a theological book. These people do not have complete faith in our *Lord*. They believe in man before Christ. If they are Christians, they should be thankful for grace!

Transformation to Eternal Life

As we know it, these times were planned from the beginning of time. The Olivet Discourse was spoken of by Jesus. This happened at the beginning of the week, when Christ was crucified. Matthew chapter 24, Mark chapter 13, and Luke chapter 21 all tell the same story. Daniel's prophecy of the abomination of desolation and Revelation show us the rest of the story. September 24, 1950, marks the day when Yevea, the original Greek word translated as *generation*, started. This date is significant as it marks the beginning of a new era in the biblical timeline. Matthew 24:29 events happened on September 24, 1950. This earmarks the end-times, the beginning of a nonreversible time clock. From the start of the generation through the generation's length, the prophecy states Christ will return. The length or duration of that Yevea or generation is spoken of in Psalm 90:10 as seventy years, but if by strength, eighty. Then knowing a man is eighty until he turns eighty-one makes you factor in that extra year. Jesus speaks this prophecy in His words; the only thing that confines Christ is His words. Not to come true would make God untruthful, which is impossible.

Revelation takes the ball from there and shows us Christ's Second Coming (chapter 19). The millennium period was a one-thousand-year reign of Jesus, ruling as King—the great white throne of Judgment. Satan and the unsaved are judged by their works at the great white throne of judgment. All judged at the great white throne are put into hell for eternity. A new heaven and a new earth are formed in Revelation chapter 21. A new Jerusalem is also in chapter 21. But God planned to come full circle, back to the garden, where everything was very good.

A chapter-by-chapter explanation of Revelation is somewhat more straightforward to understand than the complicated version that most theologians discuss.

- Chapter 1 is an introduction that shows Jesus Christ as King, Lord of lords, and master of all creation.
- Chapters 2 and 3: There are seven letters to seven churches. Seven, biblically, indicates a period of perfect time. Each letter is a period of the church age, from Jesus's resurrection until the Rapture, called the Age of Grace. We are currently at the end of the seventh letter to the Church of Laodicea.
- Chapter 4, verse 1: "And this I looked, and, behold, a door opened in Heaven: and the first voice What I heard was as if it were of a trumpet talking with me, Which said, come up Hither and I will show these things which must be here-after." This verse symbolizes the Rapture or taking away of the church or Christ's bride. Notice that Christ's voice was like a trumpet. First Thessalonians 4:16 describes what happens at the beginning of the Rapture: "For the Lord Himself shall descend from Heaven with a shout, with the voice of the Archangel, and with the Trump of God: and the dead in Christ shall rise first."
- Chapter 4–5: the twenty-four elders with gold crowns are symbolic of the church in heaven, after they were judged and given rewards in heaven, as the gold crowns are rewards given to the priests or elders.
- Chapter 6 is the beginning of the Tribulation period with the opening of the seals; the seals are the deed to the world, as Christ is taking it back from Satan.
- Chapters 6–19 explain what happens during a seven-year tribulation period: three and a half years, then the abomi-nation of desolation, then three and a half more years called the great Tribulation period or Jacob's trouble. But wait, Matthew 24:22 states, "And except those days be short-ened, there should be no flesh be saved; but for the elect's

sake, those days shall be shortened." Possibly shorter than seven years.

- Chapter 19 also includes Christ's return to earth, or the Christian's Second Coming. This will be Judaism's first coming of the Messiah, symbolized in Joseph's life as his brothers come to him to be saved from the famine in Egypt. Christ's first coming was when Joseph's brothers sold him into slavery.
- Chapter 20: Christ tells an angel to chain the devil and locks Him in a pit for one thousand years, during which Christ will reign on earth as King, high priest, and ruler over all—*the millennium period.* At the end of the millennium, the devil or Satan will be loose for a short time, bringing the unsaved to fight one last battle with Christ; He conquers all evil and extinguishes it from the earth. A great white throne, where the judgment of all unsaved from the beginning of creation will be judged and thrown into the lake of fire
- Chapter 21: There's a new heaven and new earth, where all tears are wiped away. Holy Jerusalem descends out of heaven from God. Jerusalem's size and its construction are all shown in chapter 21.
- Chapter 22: The ending chapter of a fantastic book of books, what we call the Bible, and also the Word, which is also Christ Himself. This shows a complete, full circle from the beginning of creation in the garden, when everything was very good. Again, we find ourselves in a perfect place where sin is not, darkness is not, and the light of God shines continually. Evil is defeated and is no more.

The end, from the beginning of the Yevea or generation, is laid out for us. It is a blessing to all who are circumcised by the spirit and a terrible warning to all who are not. Pray for the unsaved, for Jesus said, Whosoever believeth in me shall not perish but have eternal life.

Even if you find yourself still here after the Rapture, there is hope for you. Though it may be challenging without the restraint of evil, there is still a path to salvation. The Antichrist's deception and the mark of the beast are trials, but with unwavering faith, you can still find your way to heaven.

How simple it is now to merely have *faith*! In the face of these prophecies and events, faith is our guiding light, our source of strength, and our assurance of salvation. Let this simplicity of faith uplift and encourage you in your journey.

Epilogue

Why was this book written? Was it to instill fear in the world, or was it to prepare it? The true purpose is to reveal that September 24, 1950, was the pivotal moment, the dawn of the transition from this world to an eternal one. This date, September 24, 1950, is not just a random day but the very beginning of the generation foretold by Christ in the Olivet Discourse.

If you are a faithful Christian with a circumcised heart—that's to say, you have been baptized by the Spirit—you then have the Holy Spirit residing in your heart. If that's all that's true, you have nothing to worry about. It would help if you had a joyful anticipation of the taking away or Rapture happening. But remember, you should also have a burning desire to inform those who do not have the Holy Spirit in their hearts. This is not just a desire but a responsibility that should motivate you. After the Rapture, where Christ takes the church, His bride, out of the world, those left behind will experience a Tribulation period of possibly seven years. The length is in question, as Matthew 24:22 indicates that even the elect would not be saved if the time wasn't shortened. The events of September 24, 1950, were the only things that happened that matched up with Scripture. I would not be writing this book. It's a fantastic combination of events that shows its validation.

Let's list those events:

1. September 24, 1950, Black Sunday, a string of events that match Matthew 24:29.
2. The dates September 24–26 match Daniel's prophecy of the abomination of desolation, where Jesus spoke in Matthew 24:15.

3. The signs of the sun and the moon indicate God's hand is there to guide.

    a. The tetrads in the Reformation period, the 1900s, and the 2000s *all* showed God's hand.
    b. Total solar eclipses on Rosh Hashanah and lunar eclipses on Jewish festivals in 1949–1950.
    c. Tetrads that define the seasons of the generation, four in a row (Psalm 104:19), God appointed the moon for seasons.

4. Thomas Lynn Burrows was born that day, September 24, 1950.

    a. Thomas's family life shows God had this purpose for him.
    b. Numbers lining up with his family.
    c. The blessings he has had through his career and life.
    d. The correlation between his family and that of Abraham's, Joseph's, and Noah's in Scripture.
    e. The connection between Patricia's first husband's family and mine is uncanny.

5. James Ussher, author of *The Annals of the World* from the early 1600s. The book is a study dating back to the beginning of creation, which notes that the Sunday after the fall equinox was the start of creation, September 24, 1950, the Sunday after the fall equinox.
6. The understanding of the fig tree parable, Luke 8:10, tells us that Jesus speaks in parables to hide from those He wishes to hide. It shows He has chosen to show me the Scripture and the parable.
7. The understanding that Matthew chapter 24 was not in chronological order or verse-by-verse explanation.
8. In 2019, we moved from Reno, Nevada, to Hiawassee, Georgia. I was and still am studying September 24.

9. I was praying for confirmation of the truth God was showing me when He gave me a license plate, CAM1950. *Cam* is the Greek word for *go boldly*, as it was used to describe how Joseph of Arimathea walked boldly into Pilate and the number 1950 is the year of my birth and the year the generation began.

I boldly declare this to be an accurate assessment of God's plan. The generation, the tabernacle, and the Jewish calendar at 6028 years from Adam's creation all hit the same mark. Please encourage the lost souls that our incredible Savior has given it all for all of us. I feel chosen, but not special. As it is, Jesus plus nothing equals everything. It's all in His hands. The unsaved are being blinded by the god of this world (Satan), as in 2 Corinthians 4:4: "In whom the god of this world hath blinded the mines of them which believe not, lest the light of the glorious gospel of Christ, who is the image of God, should shine on them."

It is interesting that four has the meaning of world biblically, and this verse is 4:4.

Go spread the gospel, the free gift of salvation to the unbeliever.

References

Biblical Mathematics by Ed Vallowe
Harrisburg Patriot News
Jesusplusnothing.com website
Eclipsewise.com
Wikipedia for Sept 24 1950

About the Author

Thomas Lynn Burrows is nothing but a common Farm Boy Blessed. My life has been amazing in that God has had His Hand on me from conception, of which I show proof. My birth date is the beginning of the End of the world as we know it. Better stated the beginning of the transformation of the earth as prophesied. I've been on a 30-year journey guided by the Holy Spirit, as in the movie *ET* where the Reese's Pieces were left for a trail. The Holy Spirit has left bits of information for me to follow. This book is that journey. Please read and make a commitment of faith to Christ and avoid the Tribulation.